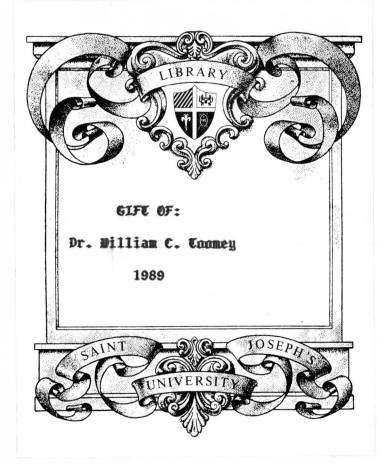

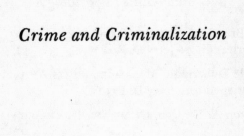

Crime and Criminalization

Viewpoints in Sociology

Lee Braude, A SENSE OF SOCIOLOGY
 (series editor: Jerry D. Rose)

Lucile Duberman, MARRIAGE AND ITS ALTERNATIVES
 (series editor: Jerry D. Rose)

Clayton A. Hartjen, CRIME AND CRIMINALIZATION

Crime and Criminalization

Clayton A. Hartjen

PRAEGER PUBLISHERS
New York • Washington

Published in the United States of America in 1974
by Praeger Publishers, Inc.
111 Fourth Avenue, New York, N.Y. 10003

© 1974 by Praeger Publishers, Inc.

Library of Congress Cataloging in Publication Data

Hartjen, Clayton, 1943–
  Crime and criminalization.

  (Viewpoints in sociology)
  Bibliography: p. 197.
  1. Crime and criminals.   2. Criminal justice, Administration of.
3. Corrections.   I. Title
[DNLM: 1. Crime.   2. Criminal behavior.   HV6080   H329c   1974]
HV6025.H32   364   74-741
ISBN 0-275-51560-3
ISBN 0-275-84950-X (pbk.)

Printed in the United States of America

TO
Sandy

Acknowledgments

No book is ever the product of a single person's efforts. The present volume is no exception. Although any expression of gratitude somehow seems inadequate, I would like to thank a number of individuals in whose debt I stand. My wife, Sandra J. Hartjen, more than anyone else made this book a possibility. Lucille Duberman and Nicholas M. Regush have been constant sources of encouragement and support. Gladys S. Topkis, my editor at Praeger Publishers, contributed more than her considerable editorial abilities. Edward Sagarin offered many useful suggestions. My former teachers, Don C. Gibbons and Richard Quinney, from whose work I have drawn liberally, remain today, as in the past, symbolic mentors, sources of inspiration, and friends. I credit all these people with generating this volume. I cannot blame any of them for its defects.

Contents

I

Crime: A Matter of Definition

ASSUME THAT WE ARE IN A BANK. A man approaches the teller and hands her a slip of paper. She, in turn, hands him a sum of money, and he proceeds to leave the premises.

Nothing in particular has occurred. The man has simply cashed a check or made a withdrawal. It happens all the time.

But now suppose we learned that the piece of paper was neither a check nor a withdrawal slip. In fact, the man never even had an account with the bank. Rather, he had handed the teller a note stating that he had a gun and would shoot if she didn't hand over the money in her drawer.

Now the event takes on an entirely different character. We have just witnessed a holdup. A crime has occurred before our very eyes. The event that we considered of little significance is revealed to be something quite different from what we had assumed it to be. It has been transformed into something worthy of concern.

What differentiates the two types of events? In both cases a sum of money was transferred. In both cases this happened simply in response to some writing on a piece of paper. Obviously the event we observed was a crime. But on what grounds can we make that statement? Because the man possessed a gun? Because

1

he didn't have an account with the bank? Because he neglected to use the standard withdrawal form? What, in short, do we mean by the word "crime"?

To the layman, and to most criminologists, the word "crime" refers to a particular kind of behavior. Rape, robbery, disorderly conduct, embezzlement, and a host of other acts come to mind.

But if we are to investigate a phenomenon called "crime" scientifically, we need to be more precise as to just what is meant by that term. Our first task, therefore, is to define crime. This is not so simple as it might appear to be, for a large number of alternative definitions are available. Even social scientists do not agree as to its meaning. The phenomena we study as the subject matter of criminology depend on the definition we choose.

Most definitions of crime take one of two major approaches—the *behavioral* or the *labeling* perspective.

CRIME AS BEHAVIOR

Behavioral definitions of crime tend to differ depending on the role they give to criminal law. Advocates of the "sociological" or "normative" approach exclude almost totally any reference to criminal law in their definitions of crime. Their argument is based largely on the premise that scientific criminology should have universal applicability—that its range of subject matter should not be limited by either time or place. The law, they say, is too relative and unstable to form an adequate standard for scientific inquiry. The proper focus of attention should be on a more general category of behavior—behavior that violates "conduct norms." Since every society has rules, or norms, designed to control the behavior of its members, the study of crime, according to this school, is the study of those activities that violate socially prescribed standards, whether or not that behavior happens to break some criminal law (Sellin, 1938:32).

The focus of this school is on antisocial conduct, wherever and whenever it occurs. Incest, for example, appears to be universally abhorred and would therefore be included in a sociological investigation of crime. Similarly, such diverse activities as homicide, cheating on examinations, income-tax evasion, and simple breaches of etiquette, such as belching at a formal dinner party, would all be proper topics for criminological inquiry.

More recent variants of the normative approach expand this list even further. Some writers have argued, for example, that a truly humanistic criminology would direct its attention to acts that violate basic human rights. Hence, criminologists should investigate "racism," "sexism," "imperialism," and the like (Schwendinger and Schwendinger, 1970).

These "sociological" definitions of crime rarely receive serious attention these days. Most criminologists would probably agree that criminologists should investigate a somewhat more limited area of inquiry than the normative approach would suggest. Some criminologists argue that a definition of crime that centers on the criminal law would best serve the interests of criminology and that norm-violating activity not covered by the criminal code should be left to the more general study of social deviance.

The central theme of "legal" definitions is quite simple: crime is any act that violates a criminal law. Indeed, as some proponents of this view suggest (e.g., Jeffrey, 1956), crime could not exist at all were it not for criminal law. After all, it is criminal law that gives behavior its quality of criminality.

There are various definitions that share this emphasis on criminal law. According to some definitions, any act that violates the criminal code—that is, any form of behavior designated by law as socially harmful and for which a penalty is prescribed—can be considered a crime and a proper subject of sociological scrutiny, whether or not some formal declaration that a law has been broken has been made by the courts. For example, one of the more popular definitions expressing this view suggests that the "essential characteristic of crime is that it is behavior which is prohibited by the State as an injury to the State and against which the State may react, at least as a last resort, by punishment" (Sutherland, 1949:31).

Other writers have argued that, since we have no way of deciding who or what is criminal until some person has been officially processed by the courts, criminology should restrict its attention to individuals who have been formally convicted by the courts as criminals. Korn and McCorkle (1959:46), for instance, have argued that an act should not be considered a crime until the actor is actually convicted of violating some law and punished. Similarly, Paul Tappan (1947) urges that only those who have been adjudged as criminal by the courts should be so considered. From this perspective, crime exists only when such a designation has been handed down by judicial authorities—that is, when some act has been officially identified as in violation of the law. A person can be considered a criminal only when and if legal authorities have ruled that he is responsible for breaking some part of the criminal code.

Before an act can be legally defined as a crime, at least theoretically, five conditions must be met: (1) An act must take place that involves harm inflicted on someone by the actor; (2) the act must be legally prohibited at the time it is committed; (3) the perpetrator must have criminal intent (*mens rea*) when he engages in the act; (4) there must be a causal relationship between the voluntary misconduct and the harm that results from it; and (5) there must be some legally prescribed punishment for anyone convicted of the act (Savitz, 1967:10-13).

Obviously, not all those who break criminal laws are caught and convicted, much less punished. Many acts that could be considered crimes are rarely submitted to the test of criminal prosecution. What meaningful conclusions can we reach about criminal behavior, therefore, if we are to study only those persons who are convicted of wrongdoing? Even the most avid legalist would not limit his conclusions only to adjudicated criminals. In most cases, persons judged as criminals simply serve as samples for study. Like the normative approach, the legal perspective of crime has the underlying objective of studying rule-violating behavior. Legal definitions of criminal behavior, therefore, differ from normative definitions only in the types of rules involved.

One of the problems with both the normative and most legal views of crime is the emphasis they place on behavior. This emphasis has led criminologists to investigate criminal phenomena from a single conceptual point of view. Most of the research in criminology taking "criminal behavior" as its central object of inquiry is oriented toward causal factors. Criminologists following these approaches have been interested mainly in explaining, predicting, and controlling criminal conduct. The questions they have addressed have been concerned largely with the behavior and characteristics of lawbreakers. Who violates the law? Why do they do it? How can crime be prevented? How can the criminal be rehabilitated? These and similar questions have largely shaped our knowledge and understanding regarding criminal phenomena. We know a good deal about lawbreakers but relatively little about other aspects of crime. Having directed attention to the criminal and the causes of criminal behavior, the behavioral approach to crime has obscured the relevance of other phenomena of interest to criminology.

Several criminologists, however, have taken issue with behavioral definitions in general. Some have suggested that behavioral definitions that focus attention on the criminal are conceptually restrictive. Other criminologists have contended that behavioral definitions perpetrate a misconception of crime, since they claim that the search for causal explanations of crime is little more than an exercise in futility. And finally, a few writers have voiced concern over the moral implications of contemporary criminology (see Gibbons and Jones, 1971).* In response to these objections, a number of alternative definitions of crime have been formulated.

CRIME AS A LABEL

There is no intrinsic reason for a definition of crime to be restricted to a behavioral conception. In fact, there is no intrinsic reason to include any reference to behavior in a definition of crime. A number of criminologists view crime as a consequence of social interaction, a result of a process that involves both the "rule violator" and others (e.g., the community, the police, the courts) who see the person's behavior as criminal. Crime, according to this view, is essentially a label attached to a person's behavior by others. Behavior may be defined or labeled as crime, but it is not this behavior in itself that constitutes crime. Rather, the behavior is criminalized—transformed into criminal behavior —by a process of social ascription (Turk, 1969). The behavior labeled criminal by agents of the law should be of interest to criminology. But the *process* and *conditions* of defining (criminalizing) persons and their conduct should also be central objects of criminological study.

Although several definitions of crime embodying this view

* This point is discussed in Chapter 8.

are available, they all share the central idea that no act is innately criminal, that the criminal character of behavior is the product of an interpretation of an individual's conduct made by some person or persons in a position to make this designation. An act is not automatically a crime. Someone in a position to make such a decision must first proclaim that the conduct in question violates some criminal law, that the act is an illegal one. Hence, any definition of crime must include some reference to the process of social labeling.

The basic notion of labeling has been aptly expressed by Howard Becker:

> Deviance is *not* a quality of the act the person commits, but rather a consequence of the application by others of rules and sanctions to an "offender." The deviant is one to whom that label has successfully been applied; deviant behavior is behavior that people so label. [Becker, 1963:9.]

Crime, in brief, is not something the observer beholds. It inheres in the perception of the beholder.

Other writers have made similar observations. Austin Turk (1969:10), for example, suggests that crime should not be viewed as some form of behavior; rather, he suggests (p. 25) that criminality is a social status defined by the way in which an individual is perceived, evaluated, and treated by legal authorities. More recently, Richard Quinney (1970a:7) has defined crime as a "legal category" assigned to a person's conduct by authorized agents. A person becomes a "criminal" when others ascribe this status to him. The basis for making this assignment is the official judgment of legal authorities that the person has committed a criminal act. Crime, in short, is the "result" of some official judgment, a decision and proclamation, made by legal authorities.

Many of the labeling definitions of crime still include a behavioral component insofar as they refer to the definition of conduct. But these approaches shift the focus of emphasis from the violations of rules to the designation of specific behavior as rule-breaking conduct. Whereas behavioral definitions lead one to investigate rule-breaking activity, the labeling perspective leads one to study the responses of legal authorities. Rules, in the labeling perspective's view, are one set of grounds for applying the label "criminal" to a person. But the rule-violating behavior to which this label is applied is not in itself "criminal conduct." The essential point is that crime is not something in the behavior of rule-breakers, regardless of the types of rules one may employ to make that designation. Crime is found in other people's perceptions and evaluations of, and responses to, persons deemed to be rule-breakers. Crime, in this view, can be said to exist only when someone makes a declaration and imposes that judgment on a particular person.

If, then, it is not what people do but how they are perceived and evaluated by others that constitutes crime, it is not what people do but how they are treated by others that provides the subject matter for criminology. Indeed, a person may never do anything illegal and still acquire a social identity as a criminal. On the other hand, most citizens probably break a criminal law at some time in their lives and are not perceived as criminals. Lawbreaking behavior, thus, provides but one dimension of a definition of crime. If we combine this dimension with the perceptions of others, we have four as opposed to two theoretical possibilities, as Figure 1 shows. People are not merely criminals and noncriminals. They are not merely lawbreakers and non-lawbreakers. They are also perceived as wrongdoers or not so perceived.

	Nonlawbreaking Behavior	Lawbreaking Behavior
Perceived as Criminal	I Falsely Accused	II Criminal
Not Perceived as Criminal	III Noncriminal	IV Secret Criminal

Source: Adapted from Becker (1963:20).

FIGURE 1: Types of Crime

In the past, criminologists who have concerned themselves only with the legal/illegal behavior of persons have been content to base their knowledge about all criminals, including those who are not officially designated as lawbreakers (category IV), on their study of perceived criminals (category II). The assumption has been that a large number of people violate criminal laws every day, but that most of them are never caught or prosecuted and hence are never officially labeled "lawbreakers." It is almost impossible to obtain a sample of these "secret" criminals to study. By studying adjudicated criminals, it is hoped, we will be able to gain more or less accurate information about criminals in general. The problem, of course, is that we can never be sure of the extent to which perceived criminals are representative of all lawbreakers, so that we can never be sure just how accurate our conclusions are.

A person who has not been defined as a criminal by others is, for all intents and purposes, a "noncriminal," regardless of his behavior. At least as far as society is concerned, the individual's social identity has not been altered. We would still hold the same opinion of him we always held; we would not behave differently toward him. It is only when the person is socially judged as being somehow different from what we once assumed him to be that we have reason to alter our conduct toward him. The social acquisition of a criminal identity is but one of a large number of occasions for treating a person differently. It is by the alteration of our conduct toward such a person that he is relegated to the social category "criminal."

Sociologically, then, the perceptual dimension is the primary one. The social reality we are about to investigate is the reality created and lived by the members of the groups being studied. The reality we investigate as crime must, therefore, be the reality created by societal members in the course of living their everyday lives. In this light, we can define crime as a *socially recognized status constructed by societal members or their authorized agents in the course of labeling someone as a criminal.* The sociological reality of crime exists, very simply, only when members select others of their group to populate the social status "criminal."

THE CRIMINALIZATION PROCESS

Definitions are neither right nor wrong. They are only more or less useful. The adequacy of a definition depends on its usefulness and the order of phenomena it leads one to investigate. The scientific significance of a definition rests on the types of questions to which it directs attention. Whereas the behavioral conception of crime directs criminologists toward the criminal offender and the causes of his conduct, the labeling view, while not totally ignoring the behavior of lawbreakers, relegates their activity to a subsidiary position. Rather than attempt to explain why people break the law, many criminologists today address the procedures, grounds, and policies involved in defining or labeling any person's conduct a crime. The central question is not why some people break the law while others do not. It is, rather, why some people's conduct is defined as crime and that of others is not. In short, it is not the criminal character of behavior that is of interest to criminology but the process of criminalizing behavior (Turk, 1969).

This concern requires that the attention of criminology shift from the violator of criminal law to the criminal-justice system and the interrelationships between the perception of crime, the administration of criminal law, and society in general. A sociological description of crime involves, therefore, an analysis of the criminalization process and the conditions that underlie the administration of criminal justice—the mechanisms involved in creating the social reality of crime.

This definition of crime implies that crime is far from absolute. I do not mean by this simply that criminal activities differ from one society to another. Nor do I mean that crime is relative to different legal systems. What I mean to imply is that crime is not something that can be observed existing in-the-world. Crime is not a "thing" one apprehends in the same way that one observes a tree or a table. Rather, crime is a construct, an image, created by social actors. It is one possible conception men hold "of-the-world." Crime is not an aspect of our experienced reality but one of many possible interpretations men make of reality experiences. In this sense, crime involves a choice. Its existence implies that the decision has been made to treat reality experiences in a particular way. The problem for the sociologist is to describe how and on what grounds members of society make this decision—in short, the *process* by which their conception of reality is transformed into actuality. The following chapters of this book focus on how behavior is criminalized by analyzing the factors and conditions that underlie the production of criminally defined persons. But before we begin that inquiry, some comments on the general nature of the process are in order.

Crime is innately political. For one thing, the very possibility of crime depends on a political process: the legislative process responsible for the creation of criminal laws. I do not mean to imply here that crime owes its existence to criminal law. Law is not a cause of crime, even though it is doubtful that behavior could be labeled criminal without the law. What I mean is that law provides a standard, a way of judging others as criminals, of transforming an instance of conduct into a criminal act. Although the majority of criminal laws are actually enforced only rarely, the mere existence of some rule furnishes an opportunity for labeling behavior as crime.

Moreover, law supplies authority, a kind of court of last appeal, for transformation activity. Insofar as law is enacted in the name of the group and is invoked on behalf of the group, law serves to justify the apprehension, prosecution, and punishment of our fellow men. Theoretically it is the group that is punishing its own. The group speaks with an authority and a power greater than those of any individual member. Also, since the law is said to codify and systematize the wishes and desires of the group, it stands above the desires and claims of any individual.

Law, as a result, has come to serve a dual function in society. First, it provides the means of registering, signifying, degrading, and stigmatizing (Matza, 1969:159) someone as a criminal, and then, it provides itself with its own justification. Law supplies the *means* and the *authority* to criminalize the behavior of another. Any analysis of crime must begin, therefore, with a discussion of the nature and origins of criminal law.

Crime is political in a second sense as well. Whereas the criminal code furnishes the ultimate grounds for criminalization, the application of these grounds is also a political act in that it involves and requires the employment of power; the power to translate legal rules into action, the power to impose one's will on others, the power to define and enforce one's definition of another's conduct as illegal.

As an inherently political phenomenon, crime is ultimately an expression of group conflict and interest. Indeed, the actual formulation of criminal laws is itself an expression of a basic conflict between the interests of differing groups. Those individuals and groups powerful enough to have their interests legitimized in law have the power to force their will upon others, to forge and enforce public policy (Quinney, 1970a:15-23).

Many criminal laws, of course, reflect the interests of the entire society, such as laws prohibiting murder, robbery, rape, and the like. But it is not yet clear whether, or to what extent, the *application* of these laws reflects political (power) interests. Some laws are enforced more frequently and more rigorously than others. In fact, a number of laws are never subjected to enforcement. Moreover, some groups appear to be likely to have their behavior controlled by legal authorities, whereas others seem to be virtually immune from criminal prosecution. Unless one is willing to assume that law-enforcement agents can apply some magic formula to gauge the opinions of the public they serve, unless one is willing to assume that citizens unanimously agree on what laws are to be enforced and how enforcement is to be carried out, unless one is willing to assume that blacks, the poor, urbanites, and the young are actually more criminalistic than everyone else, it must be concluded, at least, that discriminatory law enforcement is a result of differences in power and that actual decisions as to which and whose behavior is criminal are expressions of this power. One need only ask himself why some laws, such as those protecting the consumer from fraud, go largely unenforced while the drug addict, for example, is pursued with a paranoiac passion.

It is clear that illegal behavior is not automatically transformed into criminal conduct. Many acts violate the law, but relatively few receive official scrutiny. In fact, forms of behavior have relative probabilities of being defined as illegal. Further, acts differ in their probabilities of being treated as crimes. Law enforcement is by no means a random enterprise. Acts that are likely to be treated as criminal are those that conflict with the interests of groups in a position to dictate enforcement policy. Hence, the people who typically engage in such conduct are more likely to find themselves subjected to judicial processing than are those whose interests are reflected in criminal law (Quinney, 1970a:18). Hippies, blacks, radicals, young people, and the poor are among the most obvious. If law serves to justify criminal prosecution,

FIG. 2   A GENERAL VIEW OF

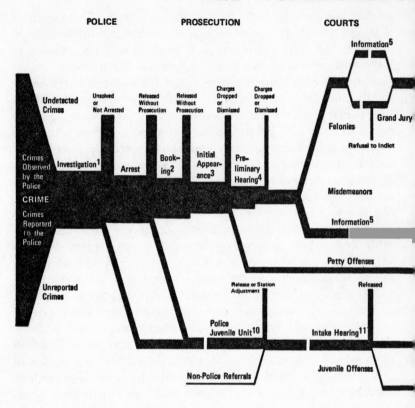

POLICE   PROSECUTION   COURTS

Information⁵

Undetected Crimes | Unsolved or Not Arrested | Released Without Prosecution | Released Without Prosecution | Charges Dropped or Dismissed | Charges Dropped or Dismissed

Crimes Observed by the Police

Investigation¹   Arrest   Booking²   Initial Appearance³   Preliminary Hearing⁴

Felonies   Grand Jury

Refusal to Indict

CRIME

Crimes Reported to the Police

Misdemeanors

Information⁵

Petty Offenses

Unreported Crimes

Release or Station Adjustment   Released

Police Juvenile Unit¹⁰   Intake Hearing¹¹

Non-Police Referrals   Juvenile Offenses

¹May continue until trial.

²Administrative record of arrest. First step at which temporary release on bail may be available.

³Before magistrate, commissioner, or justice of peace. Formal notice of charge, advice of rights. Bail set. Summary trials for petty offenses usually conducted here without further processing.

⁴Preliminary testing of evidence against defendant. Charge may be reduced. No separate preliminary hearing for misdemeanors in some systems.

⁵Charge filed by prosecutor on basis of information submitted by police or citizens. Alternative to grand jury indictment; often used in felonies, almost always in misdemeanors.

Procedures in individual jurisdictions may vary from the pattern shown here. The differing weights of line indicate the relative volume of cases typically disposed of at various points in the system.

THE CRIMINAL JUSTICE SYSTEM*

CORRECTIONS

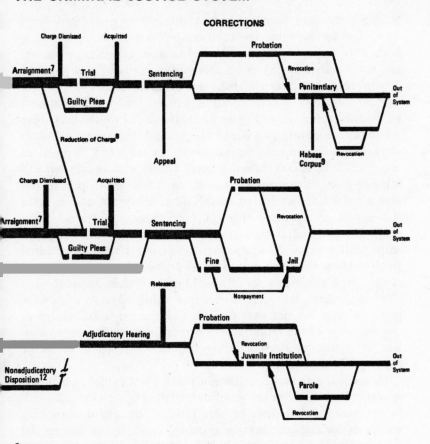

[6] Reviews whether government evidence is sufficient to justify trial. Some states have no grand-jury system; others seldom use it.

[7] Appearance for plea; defendant elects trial by judge or jury (if available); counsel for indigent usually appointed here in felonies. often not at all in other cases.

[8] Charge may be reduced at any time prior to trial in return for plea of guilty or for other reasons.

[9] Challenge on constitutional grounds to legality of detention. May be sought at any point in process.

[10] Police often hold informal hearings and dismiss or adjust many cases without further processing.

[11] Probation officer decides desirability of further court action.

[12] Welfare agency, social services, counseling, medical care, etc., for cases not requiring adjudicatory handling.

*Source: The President's Commission on Law Enforcement and Administration of Justice, *The Challenge of Crime in a Free Society* (Washington, D.C.: U.S. Government Printing Office, 1967), pp. 8-9.

behavior that has been defined by the law as prohibited offers an excuse for invoking the criminalization process. Although it is their behavior that is ostensibly being questioned, people are not necessarily selected to fill the role of criminal solely on the ground that they have violated some criminal code.

How are people selected to fill the criminal role? What happens to them in the process? Figure 2 vividly demonstrates that there are many routes into and out of the judicial machinery. All along the line decisions are made, judgments are rendered, dispositions are given. Who makes these decisions? Under what conditions will a judge place one person on parole, send another to prison, and give a third a suspended sentence? What difference does it make if a person receives one or another of these dispositions? What effect does a criminal identity have on a person and his relationships with others? To what extent does our system of criminal justice reflect the public's attitudes? Indeed, how well-informed is the populace about its criminal-justice system anyway?

These and similar questions are now being asked by criminologists. Answers are not easy to find. Criminology's knowledge of the workings of the criminalization machinery is limited at best. But an understanding of crime requires that these issues be explored in some depth.

In summary, the criminalization process is a twofold phenomenon that involves both the grounds for labeling activity and labeling procedures. To describe this process requires investigating the bases for constructing the criminal label, by addressing the issue of law and what is involved in the formulation of criminal laws. Secondly, the actual conditions, circumstances, and procedures surrounding the labeling process can be analyzed by describing the administration of justice in detail. In line with this discussion, the classes of people that are subjected to judicial handling and what effects this handling has on their lives and on society are to be investigated.

But the criminalization process is more than a conglomerate of grounds and procedures. It is a dynamic enactment of a conceptual reality. It both reflects and reinforces a dyadic view of the world; a view that places God and the Devil, right and wrong, good and evil, the law-abider and the lawbreaker on opposite sides of a moral chasm. Without this ideology the criminal-justice system would probably be unnecessary; at least, it would be absurd. But because society does have a system (a process) that dichotomizes the world in moral terms—a system that actually "discovers" criminals, that uncovers and reveals evil and corruption—the conceptual assumption prerequisite to crime is sustained and perpetuated. People are convinced that crime exists because they are so successful in finding instances of it. The question is, how is behavior criminalized?

2

Creating Crime: The Nature and Formulation of Criminal Law

CRIME BEGINS WITH THE LAW. That is to say, the possible transformation of an instance of conduct into a criminal act originates with the formulation of some criminal statute. Without the law there would be no crime. Societal members may take issue with the behavior of one of their fellows. They may even go so far as to retaliate against some person whose conduct they find offensive. But in order for that person's conduct to be treated as a crime, it is first necessary that the illegal features of the behavior be so stipulated by law. It is the criminal law that dictates the criminal qualities of behavior. And it is the law that provides societal members with justified and legitimized grounds for their retaliation. The criminalization process begins, therefore, with the formulation of criminal laws.

THE NATURE OF CRIMINAL LAW

What is law? More specifically, what is criminal law? Most observers agree that law in general and criminal law in particular are but instances of a large number of forms of social control. The principal function of law is to regulate and constrain the behavior of individuals in their relationships with others. Supposedly the law is to be employed only when other control mechanisms, such as gossip, ridicule, informal coercion, and the like, fail to operate or are inadequate for the job. The law differs from other forms of social control primarily in that it is a formal system embodying explicit rules of conduct, the planned use of sanctions to ensure compliance with the rules, and a group of authorized officials designated to interpret the rules and apply sanctions to violators (Davis, 1962:43).

In modern Western society, law has been generally divided into two basic types: civil law and criminal law. Civil law consists of a body of rules and procedures intended to govern the conduct of individu s in relationship with others. Violations of civil statutes, called *torts,* are taken to be private wrongs for which the injured individual may seek redress in the courts for the harm done to him. In most cases, some form of payment is required from the offender to compensate for the injury he has caused. Ideally, this payment is equal to the harm suffered by the person bringing suit (the complainant, or plaintiff). This, for example, is the case when an individual is required to pay for the damage resulting from an automobile accident he caused. Similarly, one company might be required to pay another a sum of money for failing to fulfill the terms of a business contract. The complainant firm is thus "compensated" for the loss it may have suffered as a result of the other company's neglect or incompetence.

A crime, on the other hand, is legally a violation of the criminal code. Although a criminal act may cause harm to some individual, crimes are regarded as offenses against the state (or "the people"). A crime is a "public" as opposed to an "individual" or "private" wrong. And it is the state, not the harmed individual, that takes action against the offender. Moreover, the action taken by the state differs from that taken by the plaintiff in a civil case. Whereas, if the case involves a tort or civil injury, compensation coincident to the harm caused is levied, in the case of crime, some form of punishment is administered. Henry M. Hart, Jr. expresses this point when he says that a crime:

> . . . is not simply antisocial conduct which public officers are given a responsibility to suppress. It is not simply any conduct to which a legislature chooses to attach a "criminal" penalty. It is conduct which, if duly shown to have taken place, will incur a formal and solemn pronouncement of the moral condemnation of the community [1958:404].

Most typically, this moral condemnation is expressed in the form of unpleasant physical consequences for the person accused of committing the conduct. Both the condemnation and the consequences that follow, Hart suggests, may be regarded as constituting the punishment. Crime differs from other legal wrongs, then, basically in the type of harm (public vs. private) it represents and in the type of sanction or penalty (punishment vs. compensation) commonly inflicted for committing the act.

One of the features of law that distinguishes it from other forms of social control is a body of rules known as *procedural laws*. Particularly in the case of crime, these rules specify the conditions for and manner in which the state may proceed against an individual accused of misconduct. Trial by jury, the right to cross-examine witnesses, the right to appeal, the right to face one's accusers, and the like are all provisions contained in procedural law. Violations of these rights by the state are violations of "due process." Such violations are grounds for appeal and could lead to reversal of a conviction. The purpose of procedural law is to protect the individual from callous and arbitrary action by the state. Most of the recent controversy surrounding Supreme Court decisions regarding "no-knock" laws, wiretapping, and the like have to do with procedural matters. These are the rules that supposedly ensure both complainant (plaintiff) and defendant that some semblance of justice exists in criminal proceedings. In effect, procedural law is the law's law.

A number of attempts have been made to formulate sociologically relevant definitions of law. Most of these definitions are primarily concerned with legal codes. Law is treated as a body of rules or norms. The difficulty in defining law has typically centered on the problem of deciding on the criteria for differentiating law norms from other types of norms, particularly regarding the inclusion of some reference to state authority. Some writers have attempted to divorce law from political (or state) authority, arguing that any rule that embodies the moral fiber of the community and the violation of which provokes the members of society to take collective action is by all rights a law-norm, whether or not this action is taken by some specifically designated authority in the name of the group. Malinowski, for example, described legal norms as rules sanctioned by "a definite social machinery of binding force, based . . . upon mutual dependence, and realized in the equivalent arrangement of reciprocal services" (1926:55). It is not the power of the state, Malinowski suggests, that gives some rules the universally binding and obligatory force of laws. Rather, it is the mutual rights and obligations of societal members that underlie rules of law.

For comparative purposes, a definition of law akin to Malinowski's concept might serve adequately. At least it would permit one to include "stateless" societies within one's investigation. But for most writers, a definition of law that fails to differentiate more precisely between various forms of rules does not specify the important characteristics of law as a body of norms quite unlike other proclamations. Hoebel, for instance, suggests a definition quite at variance with Malinowski's. According to Hoebel, "A social norm is legal if its neglect or infraction is regularly met, in threat or in fact, by the application of physical force by an individual or group possessing the socially recognized privilege of so acting" (1954:28).

One objection that has been raised regarding Hoebel's definition is that it fails to distinguish between law and government. This makes it difficult to separate them for analytical purposes, because it renders meaningless the notion that government is subject to law (Schur, 1968:75). These objections, however, are inadequate. Law and government are essentially indistinguishable. Governments not only enact and enforce their own laws, but law provides them with the authority to so act. Without law, government would be impossible. Without some form of government, or at least some authorized possessors of power, law would be senseless. Quinney (1970:13) makes this point most simply and directly: "Law is the creation and interpretation of specialized rules in a politically organized society." Criminal law differs from other laws only in the sense that included within the statute is some provision for punishment to be administered in the name of the state. Law (like crime) is inherently political.

Scholarly bickering over a proper definition of law has generally failed to include a conception of the dynamic quality of law. Law is not, however, simply a body of codified (or even uncodified) statements prohibiting some acts and prescribing others. Law is not found only in the statute books or in decisions rendered by judges. Law is realized in action. The rules of law are but a guide for action. Without interpretation and enforcement, law in the books would merely gather dust on the shelves. As Hart (1958:403) suggests, law can be analyzed sociologically as a "method" or way of doing something. Law in this respect can be studied as a social process carried out by actors within situations of social interaction. Sociologically, law consists of the behaviors, situations, and conditions for creating, interpreting, and applying legal rules.

Criminal law, then, is much more than a body of specialized rules providing for the punishment of any who violate them. As it has already been suggested, crime is not located in some activity or in the rules designating some behavior as illegal. Crime is socially created by applying this judgment to some person's conduct. A step in making that assessment is to create a law specifying that some activity is illegal. The essential theoretical characteristics of such a law have been identified by Sutherland and Cressey (1966:5-9) as involving politicality, specificity, uniformity, and penal sanction. That is, laws defining conduct as criminal are ideally products of the actions of a political authority, are specific in what they describe as illegal, apply uniformly to all members of society, and include provision for some penal sanction.

Of course, whether or not we want to stipulate that these rules are created or enforced by a body that falls within some criteria designating it as a political group or are the result of some informal ad hoc procedure carried out by the group at large is really irrelevant. The character of the group that takes action against some person's conduct is significant only for the particular case being studied. In some societies no specific political body exists. The members of such a society, however, can act as a political body if they respond in concert against one of their members. The important point is that it is the act of creating some rule providing that the offender will be punished in the name of the group that generates the possibility of crime. The sociological reality of crime is located in the application of punishment, in the *act* of enforcing the rule. Criminal law provides a standard and an excuse for defining another's behavior as crime. As such it makes crime a *possible reality*. Actually employing the law to make that designation is a method of transforming a possible reality into an empirical, actual reality. How this transformation is accomplished in practice will be our concern in subsequent chapters. Where and when did it all begin? How are criminal laws formulated? To what extent and in what ways do criminal laws reflect the values, desires, and mores of society at large? These and related questions are taken up in the remainder of this chapter.

THE ORIGINS OF AMERICAN CRIMINAL LAW

Criminal law in contemporary American society is largely an outgrowth of Anglo-Saxon law as it was formulated in England between the reigns of William the Conqueror (1066-87) and Henry II (1157-89). Although modified over the course of time and in the American experience, most of the procedural and substantive features of present-day criminal law grew out of conflicts between the king, the Church and the English landed gentry from the Norman invasion of 1066 up to the death of Henry II in 1189. This period saw the idea of tribal guilt transformed into the notion of individual guilt. With this development the concept of criminal responsibility came into being. Primarily this concept arose as a coalescence of the Christian notion of individual responsibility and the secular requirements for determining guilt. Crime, equated with a sin, became a transgression against the king.

Along with this development, there arose the idea that a person could be tried only once for any single offense. Whereas the notion of criminal responsibility grew out of the union of Christian ideals and political goals, the "double jeopardy" idea was the result of the jurisdictional disputes between the king and the Church. At this time England was plagued with a multi-court system so that a person could be tried for the same offense in an ecclesiastical court, by a representative of the king, or both. Ultimately this problem was resolved in the separation of Church and state. Although American citizens tend to see this separation as essential to freedom of religion, its actual origins were the result of a more pragmatic issue and centered on the conflict of interests between the Church and the king. Primarily it concerned the distribution of power between the Church and the state. In the end the state won out. Personal transgressions came to be defined as offenses against the state, and it was the state's prerogative to punish transgressors.

The firm establishment of this idea in English criminal law was an important occurrence. Prior to that time English custom dictated that personal offenses were a highly individual matter to be dealt with by the individual who was harmed or by his family. The success of the English kings in circumventing custom not only testifies to their power and ability to consolidate their authority but also marks a turning point in Anglo-Saxon law which has yet to be changed in existing legal systems (Jeffrey, 1957).

The idea that a personal injury is an injury to the state represents more than the fact that power had become centralized in the monarchy. The concept of crime came to serve as a principal basis for exercising power. Having acquired the sole privilege of deciding what is illegal and whether any specific act actually violates the law, the state placed itself in a prime position to solidify its power. Force and coercion were necessary ingredients to acquire this resource. It was logical that the use of force to coerce compliance with the law's dictates should evolve as the right and proper means to settle disputes (Chambliss, 1969:3). Thus, the state not only acquired the right to determine what was illegal and to decide who violated the law; it also acquired the right to punish offenders for their misconduct.

Of course, this kind of power was not granted outright to the king. He had to fight for it. When William first set foot on English soil he encountered a pluralistic society. The country was divided into eight units, each of which paid homage to a different ruler. The only unifying force in the land was the Roman Church and the customary practices of the indigenous population. Having proclaimed himself "King of England," it was William's task to unify this disparate body of people under a single sovereign—himself. The legal institution as we know it today was a principal result of his actions and those of future kings in achieving that goal. Law was the means to an end. The legal institution and the concept of crime were developed to ensure that the rule of the king would not be violated.

The procedural provisions of law designed to protect the

accused from the state are basically a result of subsequent difficulty in enforcing William's proclamation. Legal features like
the separation of the legislative and judicial functions, the rules
of evidence and due process, the various writs, the right to appeal,
the roles of judge and jury, and the like can be seen largely as
compromise administrative moves evolving from a hundred years
of political disputes between the ruler and the ruled. Procedural
law was thus a pragmatically dictated result of conflicts in power
and interest.

For instance, some system had to be developed to ensure the
uniform application of the law. Hence, the king sent judges into
the countryside to enforce his peace. But it was also necessary to
legitimize the king's law and to appease the barons and the
church for their relative loss of power. By employing peers
(jurors) to decide the guilt or innocence of accused individuals,
the government could provide the legal system with an acceptable moral base. After all, it surely was not the fault of the king
if the members of one's own community found a person guilty.
The power of the government was further enhanced by the concept of the king as a sovereign. The king could do no wrong. He
was answerable only to God. To question the king was to question God. The king's law stood as the ultimate morality. Neither
it nor its implementation could be doubted. Even the Magna
Carta of 1215 (a forerunner of the American Constitution), which
attempted to place restraints on the king, did little to convert
the king's law into the people's law. It merely gave the barons
some control over the king, but the larger populace had few resources to regulate the activity of barons, much less the king.

England, of course, is not the birthplace of criminal law or of
law in general. Even though it is clear that contemporary American criminal law is largely a product of events occurring in England after 1066, the precise origin of law, much less of criminal
law, is less clear. The earliest known legal code appeared as early
as 2270 B.C. in Babylonia. The code of Hammurabi included a
section known as *lex talionis* (the law of the talon) which stipulated "an eye for an eye, a tooth for a tooth." It is significant that
this code applied only to the nobility, so that a nobleman could
punish a commoner for an offense but a commoner had no such
recourse when harmed by a nobleman.

From the time of its early formation, then, law embodied and reflected distinctions in social class and social privilege. Other early legal codes, such as of ancient Palestine, include the concept of crime. An elementary notion of crime is found in early Greek and Roman law. In both Greece and Rome, criminal law emerged as a result of political difficulties. The enactments leading to the formation of criminal law in Greece were, in part at least, attempts to solve the political crisis of the times and to rehabilitate Greek government. Criminal law was developed primarily to protect the people from the capricious activity of the state. In the case of Roman criminal law the situation, apparently, was quite the reverse: Criminal law was developed as a device to protect the state from the people (Mueller, 1955).

Several theories have been developed to explain the origins of law (Sutherland and Cressey, 1966:9–12). One theory holds that as simpler societies evolved into more complex societies, private wrongs or torts were transformed into state or social wrongs (crimes); eventually a codified system of law evolved. The problem with this theory is that it fails to specify how this occurred; nor is it likely that the correspondence between codified laws and early private morality will be empirically demonstrated.

A second theory suggests that law originated as a rational response to the problem of social order. According to this argument, as society became more complex, informal codes of conduct were supplanted by written obligations as a rational, deliberate attempt to maintain public order or to solve the problems inevitable in any social arrangement. Although the idea that law is rational and deliberate is appealing to Western minds, any familiarity with the operations of the judicial process would cause one to doubt the accuracy of this view.

In all societies certain forms of behavior and social arrangements are highly valued. Sentiments regarding this type of behavior and institutions tend to take on a moral tone. These reactions can be called the ethical values or mores of a society. Some writers contend that contemporary law (especially criminal law) represents a crystallization of these mores. Law, it is argued, developed to systematize and support moral values by giving them formal recognition.

We have already seen that the formation of criminal law was

achieved at the expense of some elements of society to the benefit of others. A fourth theory declares that criminal law is basically an expression of power struggles between various interest groups. The groups that are in control can have their will expressed in law at the expense of others. Hence, they can decide what and who is criminal. The law, thus, was but one of the tools these groups that won in the power game could use to dominate others. We will return to the last two theories later in this chapter.

Probably all these theories are at least partially correct. But it is doubtful that any single theory wholly explains the origin of criminal law, although one or another may account for the formation of any particular law or kind of law. Moreover, it is doubtful that concrete empirical support will ever be available to test the validity of any of these theories. It is difficult even to say where and when criminal law was created, so theories purporting to account for its origin are highly speculative. It would be better to concentrate research on explaining legal change and the conditions underlying the formation of specific criminal statutes or enforcement policies. The several theories mentioned above may be useful guides for this kind of inquiry.

THE FORMATION OF CRIMINAL LAWS

Little systematic research on the formulation of criminal laws has been carried out by criminologists. From the evidence that is available, it appears that laws originate in a variety of circumstances, provoked by diverse groups and forces. The research also suggests, however, that behind the formulation of any law stands some interest group that is powerful enough to have its wishes expressed in the law. As the examples discussed below demonstrate, interest groups can play more or less active roles in generating legislation. Sometimes, as with the case of marijuana laws, the interest group in question plays a direct role in initiating the legislation. Sometimes, an interest group is active in shaping the legislation to satisfy its desires even though the group had no hand in lawmaking activity; this appears to have been the case with sexual-psychopath laws. Finally, an interest group may take no active part in initiating or shaping a law, but the law is enacted in compliance with, or in light of, the interests of this group. Theft and vagrancy laws are examples.

Theft   One of the first efforts to trace the history of legal statutes is Jerome Hall's analysis of the law of theft (1952). This study documents and interprets the origins and development of modern theft laws from fifteenth-century England to the present. According to Hall, the basic elements of modern theft laws can be traced to the Carrier's Case which took place in England in 1473. This case saw the emergence of a totally new concept of theft. Over time, this concept has been preserved and today still forms the basis for laws concerning theft.

Measured against present-day ideas about theft, the circumstances leading to the decision rendered in the Carrier's Case seem simple and clear. But in 1473 it was the occasion for a great judicial debate. It appears that the defendant in the case was hired to carry bales of merchandise to Southampton. But instead, he took the bales to another place, broke them open, and absconded with the goods. Eventually he was apprehended and charged with a felony. Ultimately he was convicted of the charges. But before this could occur, it was necessary that a decision be rendered that led to major changes in the existing theft law.

Prior to this case, the necessary element of theft was trespass, which required that property be literally removed from the premises before larceny could legally have occurred. (This concept is closer to our present-day view of burglary.) Since the carrier already had the bales in his possession, technically he could not have committed trespass; hence, he was not guilty of theft. No precedent had been set to interpret the case differently, and since the facts of the case did not meet the legal requirements of the time, the judges were faced with a grave difficulty.

In the end they solved their problem by arguing that since the carrier had broken into the bales and removed their contents he had, in effect, committed trespass. Even though he had possession of the bales he did not have possession of their contents. Removal of the contents from the bales was then interpretable as an act of trespass.

By this decision, Hall suggests, the jurists opened the door to a total rewriting of theft law. A distinction was made between the concepts of "custody" and "possession." The carrier did indeed have custody of the goods, but he did not have legal possession of them. By appropriating them to his own use he had taken possession of something that was not his. A similar ruling now holds for such activities as joy riding, in which a person "temporarily" appropriates an automobile that does not belong to him for his own pleasure.

The decision reached in the Carrier's Case represented a departure from and a renunciation of precedent. At the same time, however, the actual decision formally complied with the legal standards of the time. It was, thus, a unique page in the history of jurisprudence. The question to be asked is, why was this decision made when and where it was made? For an answer, Hall turned to the events immediately preceding the case—specifically, the economic and political conditions of fifteenth-century England.

What is clear from Hall's analysis is that the problem faced by the jurists in the Carrier's Case was more a result of historical circumstances than of any peculiarities of the case itself. Had the circumstances been otherwise, no legal problem would have existed. The defendant would probably have been acquitted. But powerful forces conspired to force the decision that was ultimately reached.

At this point England and the rest of Europe were undergoing a commercial revolution. The old feudal order and agricultural economy were fast being replaced by an industrial and commercial establishment. England and the Crown were highly dependent on foreign trade. Edward IV, who was a merchant himself, had provided covenants to foreign merchants guaranteeing safe passage for themselves and their goods. It was in the King's interest to ensure favorable relationships with these merchants. Since the courts of law were subservient to the Crown, they were concerned with protecting the interests of the King. Commerce was one of these interests. Hence, the decision rendered in the Carrier's Case was clearly a move to protect the economic ventures of the Crown. Hall (1952:54) summarizes the important features of this case as follows:

> On the one hand, the criminal law at the time is clear. On the other hand, the whole complex aggregate of political and economic conditions described above thrusts itself upon the court. The more powerful forces prevailed—that happened which in due course must have happened under the circumstances. The most powerful forces of the time were interrelated very intimately and at many points: the New

Monarchy and the *nouveau riche*—the mercantile class; the business interests of both and the consequent need for a secure carrying trade; the wool and textile industry, the most valuable, by far, in all the realm; wool and cloth, the most important exports; these exports and the foreign trade; this trade and Southampton, chief trading city with the Latin countries for centuries; the numerous and very influential Italian merchants who bought English wool and cloth inland and shipped them from Southampton. The great forces of an emerging modern world, represented in the above phenomena, necessitated the elimination of a formula which had outgrown its usefulness. A new set of major institutions required a new rule. The law, lagging behind the needs of the times, was brought into more harmonious relationship with the other institutions by the decision rendered in the Carrier's Case.

The law was out of tune with the requirements of the time. Its change was, according to Hall, inevitable. We might add that it also was out of keeping with the interests of those who dominated and for whom some change in the law was desirable.

Vagrancy   Vagrancy statutes first appeared in England in 1349 (Chambliss, 1964). Originally these laws stipulated that it was a crime to give alms to any person of sound mind and body who was unemployed. The actual intent of the law, according to Chambliss, was to provide an abundant supply of cheap labor to landowners during a period when serfdom was breaking down and the available labor pool was being depleted. The prime mover behind the legislation was the Black Death, which struck England in about 1348. It is estimated that this plague caused the death of more than half of the population, severely reducing the labor force. Landowners, who were the powerful class during this period, were in a desperate situation. Something had to be done to keep the workers in the fields. Apparently pressure was put on the king by the landowners to do something to alleviate the situation. The result was the first vagrancy law.

Shortly after their enactment, the vagrancy statutes fell into disuse, although from time to time changes were made increasing the punishment for violation. In 1530, however, the statutes were reactivated with considerable alteration in both wording and intent. The emphasis now shifted to controlling "rogues," "vagabonds," and others suspected of criminal activity. As we saw in the Carrier's Case, England in the 1500s was undergoing dramatic social and economic changes. The increase in commerce and trade during this period made it necessary that some protection be offered merchants who had to run the gauntlet of highwaymen and unscrupulous carriers. The vagrancy statutes were one of the measures taken to serve this end.

Again the vagrancy laws fell into disuse, only to be revived once more in the eighteenth century. Since then the vagrancy statutes have remained virtually intact, with only minor changes from time to time directed toward clarifying and expanding the provisions of the laws. These same laws were those subsequently adopted in the American colonies. And in modern America, as in England, the central purpose of the vagrancy laws is to control criminals and other undesirables. Vagrancy statutes provide a handy excuse for apprehending a suspect when evidence of wrongdoing is lacking or hard to come by.

As Chambliss points out, vagrancy statutes, like the laws concerning theft, reflect the desires of powerful interest groups. Vagrancy laws emerged in order to provide landowners with a supply of cheap labor. When this group no longer needed cheap labor and were no longer powerful, the laws fell into disuse. Similarly, when the interests of a new power class—e.g., the mercantile class—were threatened, the vagrancy statutes were reactivated and appropriately altered to reflect the desires and needs of this group. Finally, the use of vagrancy laws in contemporary society to keep bums and other undesirables off the streets, or at least out of respectable neighborhoods, suggests the influence of middle-class desires and power to shape criminal law.

The Marijuana Tax Act   Howard Becker (1963:121–46) declared that rule creation, like rule enforcement, is an enterprising act. Rule creation and enforcement are not automatic; someone has to take the initiative to have a rule passed or applied. Behind every rule there is an entrepreneur who, for one reason or another, sought to have the rule created and by whose efforts legislation came into being. This, Becker suggests, was the case with marijuana control.

Although people noticed marijuana use as early as the 1920s, no one was much concerned, nor were any efforts made to prohibit its use. In 1937, however, the Marijuana Tax Act was passed by Congress. Ostensibly, this law was a revenue measure, imposing a nominal tax on the sale or importation of the marijuana plant. In effect, however, the law was designed to stamp out the use of the drug. But why was the law passed in 1937? Why not earlier, or later, or never?

As Becker points out, the marijuana law found firm support in the American value structure, and ample precedent had been established by the Eighteenth Amendment and the Volstead Act, restricting the use of alcohol, and by the Harrison Act of 1914, which outlawed the use of opiates. But apparently no one considered marijuana use a serious problem until the Federal Bureau of Narcotics entered the picture.

This Bureau, a division of the Treasury Department, was created as a consequence of the Harrison Act. It was the Bureau, Becker found, that supplied most of the enterprise that led to the Marijuana Tax Act. The efforts of the Bureau took two forms. First, it cooperated in developing state legislation prohibiting marijuana use. Secondly, it embarked on a strong "educational" campaign to warn the public of the "dangers" of marijuana. This was accomplished by supplying facts and figures (along with atrocity stories) to the mass media regarding the effects of marijuana. Most of the articles appearing at the time the law was passed owe their information to the efforts of the Narcotics Bureau. The goal of the Bureau was to influence the legislature to pass an act it deemed desirable both by direct pressure and by arousing the public to the dangers of marijuana in the hope that concerned citizens would pressure the Congress to do something about marijuana.

These efforts were eminently successful. The bill passed the House and Senate with little opposition. A new class of criminals was instantly created. Interestingly enough, the bill did meet some opposition before going to Congress. The manufacturers of hempseed oil objected to the wording of the bill, but they were soon pacified by alteration of a few sentences. The manufacturers of birdseed also voiced opposition to the bill once they realized that it might affect their business. They too were pacified by the stipulation that hempseeds could be imported for the purpose of manufacturing bird feed, provided that the seeds were sterilized. Marijuana smokers, the group that was most affected by this law, were not heard at the hearings. The Marijuana Tax Act is but one example of how those who are most affected are frequently the last to be consulted in the consideration of legislation.

Becker's analysis centers on the moral enterprise of the Federal Bureau of Narcotics. He implies that the director of the Bureau acted out of moral concern, seeking to outlaw marijuana use because he perceived some harm that fell within his realm. A more recent analysis of the marijuana case questions this position.

According to a study by Donald Dickson (1968), the director of the Federal Bureau of Narcotics acted more out of bureaucratic considerations than from any moral concern over marijuana use. The Narcotics Bureau was created to enforce the provisions of the Harrison Act, which was created to control the distribution of opiates, such as heroin. Since this law was vaguely worded and excluded a large portion of the addicted population (those who received their drugs from licensed physicians), the Narcotics Bureau was faced with a severely restricted scope of operations. However:

> Given the normal, well-documented bureaucratic tendency toward growth and expansion, and given the fact that the Division was a public bureaucracy and needed to justify its operation and usefulness before Congress, it would seem that increased power and jurisdiction in the area of drug control would be a desirable and, in fact, necessary goal [Dickson, 1968:149].

At first the Bureau was satisfied with arousing the public about opiates and broadening the provisions of the Harrison Act, thereby increasing its power and scope of operations. It did this by using the same tactics employed later in the case of marijuana. One result of their activities was a budgetary increase of more than 400 per cent.

In the early 1930s, however, the Bureau was faced with budgetary cuts, and with a general decline in interest and concern over drugs. It was bureaucratically essential that the Bureau find a new way to legitimize its existence. Marijuana, since it was little known and of little concern to anyone, was a perfect substitute. By 1936 the Bureau had successfully induced all 48 states to pass anti-marijuana legislation. The Bureau continued its activities until the federal marijuana act was passed in 1937. State laws, after all, do not affect the budget-demanding power of a federal organization. Like the theft laws and vagrancy statutes that came before it, the Marijuana Tax Act reflected the interests of a group that was influential enough to have its desires expressed in law.

Sexual Psychopathy It is not always necessary that some powerful interest group be directly active in order to have some statute passed in its favor. Frequently the enactment of a law is a response to general community concern. The provisions and tone of the law, however, are usually the result of some organized group's influence. This appears to have been the case with a group of statutes known as sexual-psychopath laws (Sutherland, 1950; 1950a).

Since 1937, many states have enacted these laws. Generally they provide that sexual psychopaths, defined as persons who have irresponsible sexual impulses, be confined to a mental institution for an indefinite period. Although the theoretical propositions upon which all these laws seem to be based are of dubious validity at best and even though enactment of the laws has had no impact on the incidence of sex offenses, the diffusion of sexual-psychopath laws continued unabated until the majority of the states had passed legislation of this kind. How could such laws be passed in the first place?

Sutherland's analysis of these laws shows that agitation to do something about sex offenders typically followed several bizarre and highly publicized sex crimes, especially when the victim was a child. Once public concern had been aroused and sex crimes defined as a serious threat to the well-being of women and children, efforts to enact legislation to solve the problem were soon under way. Like so many other cases, the sexual-psychopath laws are examples of the attempt to solve a social problem by legislation.

Sexual-psychopath laws were not produced automatically, however. Committees and citizen-action groups were formed to address the problem. In most cases these groups and the legislative proposals they produced were either directly or indirectly influenced by psychiatrists, which accounts for the substance of the specific laws.

As Sutherland points out, the psychiatrists were the most important interest group behind the laws. Their activity, to be sure, was consistent with their general view that sex crimes resulted from some kind of mental or emotional pathology. So the psychiatrists were not totally self-seeking in their recommendations. But they did have an economic interest in the legislation, since most laws stipulated that the diagnosis for the court must be performed by a psychiatrist. In short, the psychiatrists' standing in the community as respected, knowledgeable scientists afforded them sufficient power to sway legislators to their views.

Other Laws Examples of interest-group influence in formulating or blocking certain legislation abound. Laws governing the use of alcohol, regulations concerning sexual conduct, abortion bills, pure food and drug legislation, antitrust laws, and the like are all documented instances of interest-group activity. (See Quinney, 1970a:49–60, 65–70, 73–82, 86–94.) Even changes in existing statutes are not immune from meddling by those who see some threat or advantage in the proposed alterations, as Pamela Roby (1969) clearly demonstrated in a study of the New York State Penal Code regarding prostitution. The changes originally proposed in this law were drastically altered by the time the new statute took effect. Throughout the legislative process, various groups (e.g., the police, the New York Hotel Association, the Civil Liberties Union, the Mayor's office) were all involved in shaping the legislation to fit their interests or views.

Where does the public stand in relation to these efforts? To what extent does law reflect the interests of the public in general? Is law oriented to the general good, or is it enacted at the expense of the common citizen? Little information is available to answer these questions. Theories abound, but few studies are available to support these theories. Any statement regarding this issue can be only tentative at best.

THE LAW AND THE PUBLIC

Sutherland once said that when the mores of a society are adequate, laws are unnecessary; and when the mores are inadequate, laws are useless (see Sutherland, 1966:11). Whether or not this is, in fact, the case, the statement does point to an important issue: To what extent does law reflect the moral fiber of a community? Is law a barometer of a society's moral values? Or, conversely, is law in conflict with the customary practices of societal members? If law does indeed reflect and crystallize the mores, then, law, although substantially unnecessary, is a standard for the common good. But if law conflicts with the interests of the community at large, or of segments of the community, then law is of value only to those whose interests it serves, and becomes an instrument of repression.

Two dominant schools of thought have emerged with regard to this issue. One argues that law exists for and functions in order to secure the common good. The other suggests that law exists for and enhances the goals of only some members of society, those who are powerful enough to influence the substance of law and justice (see Schur, 1968:17–85). These contradictory views provide important reference points for understanding the legal system. A more thorough appreciation of the issues involved can be obtained by contrasting the major arguments of the two positions.

One of the best-known and most influential legal scholars, Roscoe Pound, proposed a "consensus" model of law. (See, e.g., Pound, 1942; 1959). Pound envisioned society as composed of diverse groups whose interests often conflicted but which were in basic harmony. Moreover, he argued that certain interests were essential for the well-being of society. Hence, he maintained that a reconciliation between the conflicting interests of the various groups in a society was necessary in order to secure and maintain social order. To Pound, law was a major mechanism to achieve this goal. Law, according to Pound,

> . . . is an attempt to satisfy, to reconcile, to harmonize, to adjust these overlapping and often conflicting claims and demands, either through securing them directly and immediately, or through securing certain individual interests, or through delimitations or compromises of individual interests, so as to give effect to the greatest total of interests or to the interests that weigh most in our civilization, with the least sacrifice of the scheme of interests as a whole [1943:39].

Moreover, Pound suggested, the historical development of law demonstrates a growing recognition and satisfaction of human wants or claims or desires through social control. As it has evolved over time, Pound observed, law has concerned itself with an ever wider spectrum of human interests. It has more and more come to provide for the common good and the satisfaction of social wants (Pound, 1959:47).

In short, Pound saw law as a form of "social engineering" directed toward enhancing social harmony. Thus, he encouraged the study of the "living law"—that is, the law as it actually is, "law in action," as it were. His principal goal in this inquiry was to bring the living law into greater conformity with his conception of what the law should be. The purpose of law, Pound argued, was to maintain and ensure those values and needs essential to social order, not by imposing one group's will on others, but by controlling, reconciling, and mediating the diverse and conflicting interests of individuals and groups within society. In short, the purpose of law was to control interests, not to advance those of any particular segment of society.

In sharp contrast to Pound's consensus theory, Richard Quinney (1970a:35–42) has recently postulated a "conflict" theory of law. Whereas Pound's formulation is oriented to a conception of society characterized by consensus and stability, Quinney's theory is based on a conception of society favored by a large number of sociologists (e.g., Marx, Lewis Coser, Dahrendorf). These men argue that society is typically characterized by diversity, conflict, coercion, and change. On the basis of this idea, Quinney argues that, rather than being a device to control interests, law is an expression of interests, an outgrowth of the inherent conflict of interests characteristic of society. Quinney states, "Law is a *result* of the operation of interests, rather than an instrument that functions outside of particular interests. Though law may control interests, it is in the first place *created* by interests" (1970a:35). According to this view, law is seldom the product of the whole society. Laws are created and applied by men who have the power to translate their interests into public policy. Law does not, therefore, represent a compromise of the diverse interests of a society. No matter to what extent the community may agree with the law, law in every case represents a victory of one group over another, a victory born of the conflict of interests and secured by differentials in power. Law supports some interests at the expense of others, even when those interests are those of the majority. Hence, law is inherently oppressive. Quinney (1973) goes on to suggest that reform of the legal system is not enough. The law, he says, must be removed and replaced by a new formula (or by none at all), one that ensures the rights of every man and expresses and reflects the desires of all. It is not simply that conventional judicial policies are wrong. The entire concept of law is unjust and repressive. It must, therefore, be abolished.

This is surely a utopian idea, about as probable as Pound's ideal version of the law. Quinney's suggestion would not only require drastic changes in our social system but a total reordering of the worldview on which existing legal practices are based. The notion of an ordered universe governed by natural law and of a natural progression to human history would have to be left by the wayside. In like manner, the abolition of law, or at least of the mythology of law's conciliatory role in human affairs, implies a total readjustment of our image of man and his relationships to others. Existing law is grounded on a notion that some men are vicious, self-seeking, unconstrained animals. Law exists to protect us from one another. Before the existing legal structure could be changed, this image of man would have to be washed from commonsense philosophy.

This may not be so bizarre a possibility as it might at first appear. Man's conception of himself has indeed changed in the course of time. Anthropologists have demonstrated more than once that a diversity in human consciousness exists throughout the world. Even such seemingly universal notions as time and space are culturally created artifacts of the human experience. Order produced by law is by no means a universal or even a necessary notion.

Is this in fact the case? Maybe there is a grain of truth in both perspectives. We are all aware that law sometimes serves the interests of some groups while excluding those of others. Sometimes law can indeed be unjust. Some people are falsely accused and unfairly convicted of crimes they did not commit. But, it is frequently argued, in the long run, justice is generally achieved. Most people agree with the law and with judicial practices most of the time. Most laws do reflect the community's concerns. Law may not be perfect. But it does largely reflect the mores of the times. Or does it?

We have already seen how interest-group activities are responsible for the formation of some criminal laws. Although not conclusive by any means, a number of investigations regarding public attitudes toward the law also tend to support the conflict theorists' position.

One of the first studies of this kind asked students at the University of Minnesota to choose the most serious offenses from a list of 13 minor felonies which were nearly equal in the penalties provided by California state law (Rose and Prell, 1955). The list included crimes ranging from child-beating, assault with a deadly weapon, possession of weapons, to issuing fictitious checks. Even though the penalties provided by law for these offenses were similar, the respondents produced a distinct rank ordering of offenses in terms of seriousness. Child-beating and assault were judged to be the most serious, while weapons offenses were at the bottom of the list. These judgments more often than not were at variance with judicial practices since child-beaters, for example, actually tend to receive shorter sentences than do individuals convicted of crimes viewed as less serious by the students.

In a similar study, Gibbons (1969) asked San Francisco citizens to indicate the punishment they thought appropriate for a variety of crimes ranging from second-degree murder to exhibitionism and drunk driving. Gibbons found that five of the offenses included in the FBI classification of serious crimes (murder, robbery, manslaughter, burglary, and rape) received the harshest penalties from respondents. These crimes also tend to receive the longest sentences in actual practice. But other crimes that typically receive lenient sentences (e.g., embezzlement, antitrust violation) were also judged quite serious by the respondents. Also, in a number of cases, respondents opted for penalties (usually psychotherapy) that are infrequently assigned in most criminal cases. In general, citizens appear to concur only partially with existing judicial policy.

Other studies have dealt with societal attitudes toward particular forms of criminality. For example, in a study by Rooney and Gibbons (1966), the views of San Francisco residents regarding "crimes without victims" were investigated. Respondents were asked if the laws concerning abortion, homosexuality, and drug addiction should be liberalized, kept as they were, or made more restrictive. Most respondents agreed that abortion laws should be liberalized. Since abortion law in California at the time of the study was much more stringent than what the citizens appeared to favor, Rooney and Gibbons concluded that the then current abortion laws were out of step with social attitudes. Regarding homosexuality, however, citizens tended to favor laws treating consenting homosexual conduct as a crime. Also, the respondents were distinctly opposed to any liberalization of the drug laws.

A second study of this type dealt with attitudes toward violations of the Federal Food, Drug and Cosmetic Act. In this investigation, Donald Newman (1957) asked a sample of consumers to select the penalty they thought most appropriate for misbranding, adulteration of food, and similar misconduct. The cases for study were selected from the files of a Federal District Attorney so that comparisons could be made between citizens' views and the actual penalty imposed. In most cases, the various consumers selected more severe penalties than the ones actually imposed. Yet the penalties selected by the consumers were not beyond those stipulated by law. It appears, then, that it is not the statutes but judicial practice that departs from public sentiment. Even though the penalties chosen by the citizens for these cases were harsh, they were less severe than the sentences typically dealt out to run-of-the-mill burglars, thieves, and other "criminal" types.

It would appear from the foregoing that the practice of law and the public's desires correspond only weakly. Of course, there is a good deal of variability in public sentiments. For example, Erwin O. Smigel (1956) found that respondents tended not to disapprove of those who stole from large, impersonal organizations as much as they did if the victim firm was small and personal. In another study, Smigel (1953) found that respondents scoring low in socio-economic status were favorable toward violations of unemployment compensation laws whereas those scoring higher in status disapproved of such conduct.

These and a number of similar investigations seem to support the idea that a diversity of opinion exists regarding the law. In many respects, the law is indeed out of step with public sentiment. But there also appears to be a good deal of disagreement among citizens regarding law and legal practices. Not only do citizens' attitudes toward the law differ considerably, but a good deal of variability is found in investigations regarding citizens' fear of crime and their attitudes toward crime control. The controversy over the use of the death penalty is but one example of this lack of consensus.

It is difficult to evaluate any claim regarding the relationship between law and social mores. Clearly the law does not always meet the desire of community members. But there is great diversity of moral values in modern communities. What is reprehensible to one person may be acceptable practice to another. It may be that there is some core of values that is shared by most members of society, but this has yet to be demonstrated empirically.

CONCLUSION

Criminal laws serve as criteria for criminalizing the behavior of individuals. Although the matter is far from settled, the research reported in this chapter suggests that the formulation of criminal laws stems from the conflict of interests among the various subgroups comprising society. Criminal laws not only reflect interests, but can be used to help group members obtain, establish, or protect conditions favorable to their interests. To the extent that the interests of groups are conflicting so that the enactment of certain laws benefits some groups at the expense of other groups, the resolution of whose interests are to be defended, or established as a matter of public policy ultimately depends on the differential distribution of power in society.

This is not to suggest that the criminal laws filling the statute books were mostly formulated by groups that possessed the ability to dictate public policy for purely self-serving motives. Some laws no doubt did originate in this way. But most criminal laws are probably created for the benefit of the larger community. Indeed, despite the disparity in public attitudes and opinions regarding criminal laws, probably few people would take issue with most of the laws under which they are required to live. In this regard, the entire society can be seen as the interest group whose desires are protected by law. It remains to be shown, however, to what extent this is in fact the case.

Yet some people are selected to occupy the status "criminal." Usually this happens because they are thought to have acted in ways that threaten the interests embodied in the law. Criminalization thus involves the application of criminal law to a person's behavior. *Insofar as the criteria for labeling someone a "criminal" reflect some disparity in group interests and power, that which is defined as crime and those who are selected to fill the criminal status are socially created objects of the structural characteristics of human society that produce conflict and inequitable distribution of power in society.*

3

Breaking the Law:
Theories of Crime Causation

CRIMINAL LAW IS CONCERNED with the behavior of societal members. Although a person may be prosecuted on criminal charges if he conspires with others to violate a criminal statute, he is not legally guilty of wrongdoing if he simply contemplates committing a crime. To be held legally accountable for a criminal offense, one must be shown to have acted in an illegal manner. Given the onerous consequences that could follow from committing an illegal act, the question arises as to why people break the law. Except for those, probably few, cases in which the law is violated out of ignorance or accident, what causes individuals to commit crimes? What are the factors or conditions that somehow motivate, compel, draw, or lead people into illegal activity? The attempt to answer this question is the study of crime causation, or etiology. Most of the theorizing and research in criminology has been devoted to this issue. Improper socialization, poor peer-group relations, poverty, bad home environment, psychological or physiological malfunctioning or abnormality, biological inferiority, and lack of religious training are just a few of the numerous factors that have been said to be the cause of crime. Little empirical evidence exists to support any of these claims.

To deal with the hodgepodge of explanatory assertions is itself an exhausting undertaking. The various arguments, however, can be categorized in a number of ways for purposes of discussion. In this book, the explanatory approaches are classified according to their degree of generality. Some theories address criminal behavior in *general;* others apply only to a *specific* form of criminality; a third group constructs *typologies* of crime that incorporate aspects of both concerns. A brief discussion of several approaches may serve to illuminate the main features of these types of theories.

GENERAL THEORIES OF CRIMINAL BEHAVIOR

Except for the behavior of individuals who are "obviously" sick, insane, inept, or suffering from some similar condition, popular explanations tend to group the causes of criminality within a relatively few motivational categories. Love, jealousy, hate, greed, the need to belong, overpermissiveness, and similar "reasons" fill the layman's bag of explanatory accounts. To many people, crime is a consequence of some faulty characteristic of the individual or his life experiences.

Although they are by no means contradictory to the general premise that crime stems from some deficiency of individuals, the various scientific and pseudoscientific theories of crime imply that lay explanations are wrong in that these theories usually cite quite different factors as the causes of crime. But, as we shall see, it is doubtful that science has improved much on common sense.

The Classical School Even before a science of criminology evolved, a school of thought had developed which, if not directly responsible for contemporary arguments, at least paved the way for modern criminological thinking about the causes of crime. The so-called classical school of criminology was actually the byproduct of a judicial-reform movement in eighteenth-century Europe (Vold, 1958:14–26).* Several legal scholars of the time (e.g., Jeremy Bentham, Cesare Beccaria, and John Stuart Mill) sought to correct the injustices and irrationalities of the existing legal system. Employing an odd mixture of humanism and ra-

---

* Vold's analysis of the various theories of crime is generally considered one of the outstanding references on the topic. Much of this chapter relies on Vold's summary.

tionalism, the proponents of this school reasoned that man is basically a rational animal possessing a will that enables him freely to choose courses of action. Criminal conduct must, therefore, be the result of a deliberate, rational decision to break the law. Since man also possesses the desire to achieve pleasure and avoid pain, this deliberate choice must represent a calculated move to gain that goal: crime, in other words, must provide some kind of pleasure to the criminal. It follows logically that to deter a person from criminal ways, one must administer pain of an appropriate amount and kind to counterbalance the pleasure derived from crime.

The application of pain was not considered to be unjust by these early reformers. Indeed, it was thought to be essential. Injustice occurred when the amount of pain was more than was necessary to deter the individual from breaking the law. As a result, advocates of this school attempted to develop pain scales, or "hedonistic calculi" of punishment, that identified the appropriate amount of pain to be dealt out for specific types of crime.

People might scoff at this idea today, but its vestiges still underlie Western criminal law. Punishment, in the form of prison sentences, is still administered to lawbreakers, and different amounts of punishment, as is indicated by the various penalties prescribed by law, are meted out depending on the type or degree of the crime. Indeed, neoclassical thought still forms the ideological nucleus of modern systems of criminal justice. The administration of justice in twentieth-century society actually derives from a model developed over two hundred years ago.

Innate Criminality Shortly after the revisionist moves of the classical writers, a school of criminological thought developed that still appeals to many. This approach attributes criminal conduct to biological or physiological characteristics of the criminal. The logic of this approach suggests that differences in behavior could stem from the undisputed biological differences among people. Moreover, it is argued that criminal conduct may be traced to specific biological factors that operate so as to cause individuals to break the law. Usually these factors are thought to represent biological defects of the individual. Coincident with this assertion, it has frequently been contended that to "cure" criminality it is necessary to correct or compensate for the biological or genetic defect afflicting the individual. Failing this, some writers have advocated segregation or sterilization so as not to transmit the "disease" to future generations.

A chief exponent of this school of thought, Cesare Lombroso (1836-1909), has often been credited as one of the founders of contemporary criminology. According to Lombroso, many criminals are atavists, genetic throwbacks to an earlier form of man, from which the modern *Homo sapiens* supposedly evolved. This earlier form Lombroso dubbed *Homo delinquens*. Further, Lombroso claimed that this criminal type can readily be identified by such physical peculiarities or "stigmata" as excessively long arms, unusually large or small ears, eye defects, and distinctive skull shape.

Lombroso revised his theory in later editions of his book, arguing that there are three basic types of criminals: born criminals, insane criminals, and "criminaloids." The last group appears to encompass what are today called "situational" criminals—people who are normal in all respects but are impelled to violate the law by circumstances over which they have no control.

Although Lombroso claimed to have proved his theory that a born-criminal type exists, subsequent research, primarily the studies of Charles Goring (1913:173), cast doubt on Lombroso's theories. Although Goring did not totally reject biogenic causes, he and his associates concluded that there is no such thing as a criminal type.

More sophisticated than the work of Lombroso, the related notions of the anthropologist Earnest Hooton (1939) have also failed to withstand the test of research. On the basis of anthropomorphic measurements of more than 13,000 convicts, Hooton claimed that criminals are "organically inferior," "low-grade human organisms" that are innately predisposed to criminality. He advocated total and permanent segregation of criminals as the only feasible solution to the problem.

Later efforts have also sought to relate criminal conduct to specific physical and temperament types. William Sheldon (1949), for example, identified three somatic types with corresponding temperament patterns. Although a number of attempts have been made to apply Sheldon's typology to criminal behavior, most of this research offers little support for the idea that physiological factors underlie criminal conduct. Delinquents and criminals may exhibit certain physical features that differentiate them from nonoffenders, but it can hardly be concluded from this that physical structure causes the individual to commit criminal acts. More likely than not, some people are physiologically suited for some activities, including certain kinds of crime (Glueck and Glueck, 1951). For example, large, strong, husky men are physically better suited to playing football (as they are to committing assault) than are ninety-pound weaklings. But large, strong, husky men are not disposed to playing football or committing assault *because* of their physique

A more recent version of the biogenic thesis has attempted to link violent criminal conduct to a chromosome abnormality known as the XYY pattern. Since the Y chromosome is associated with male biological characteristics, some authorities have argued that people who possess an extra Y chromosome as in the XYY pattern may tend toward pronounced aggressive antisocial conduct, which could take the form of violent criminal acts. This theory has received a good deal of attention in the mass media, and substantial research has been carried out comparing the chromosomal patterns of incarcerated criminals and samples of non-incarcerated males. So far this research has shown that a slightly larger number of incarcerated individuals have the XYY pattern. But in a review of these studies, Richard Fox (1971) suggests that the research does not support the thesis that the XYY pattern leads to aggressive behavior. In fact, Fox (1971:72–73) concluded that "the studies done thus far are largely in agreement and demonstrate rather conclusively that males of the XYY type are not predictably aggressive. If anything, as a group they are somewhat less aggressive than comparable individuals with an XY chromosomal pattern."

In spite of a large amount of research to the contrary, some criminologists still take an active interest in biogenic explanations of crime, so that the search for biological causes of criminal behavior is likely to continue for some time.

The Criminal as Sick It is common today to argue that criminal conduct is the result of serious mental pathology, or at least of some emotional or personality quirk. The dissemination of psychological teachings and the widespread attention given by the mass media to infrequent but highly bizarre forms of criminality have probably done more to popularize this view than the merits of the various arguments that support it would warrant.

Psychoanalytic and psychiatric theories of criminal behavior are too numerous and varied to be detailed in this brief discussion. Some contend that criminal conduct results from mental disorder or impairment either bordering on or representing serious psychosis (e.g., Abrahamsen, 1945). Other theories attribute criminality to neurotic tendencies or emotional disturbances of a mild variety (Glueck and Glueck, 1951). Most theories employ Freudian concepts, arguing, for example, that people break the law because of a need to act out emotional conflicts, a desire to be punished, or uncontrollable sexual impulses. Most commonly these impulses, cravings, needs, or what-have-you are attributed to faulty superego development resulting from inadequate family life or some aspect of the person's psychological development. The goal in treating an individual so afflicted is to uncover the conditions leading to his behavior rather than to focus on the conduct per se, since the behavior is regarded as but a symptom of some underlying malfunctioning.

It appears that most people favor psychological explanations of crime over alternative explanations for certain types of criminality. Run-of-the-mill acts of theft, for example, are readily understood by the common citizen on rational grounds. People steal, after all, because they need money, or because they are simply greedy.* But acts for which no rational motive can be found, like voyeurism, mass murder, and child molesting, defy explanation. People who do such things are surely not normal. Since it is difficult to pass such conduct off as an example of the "devil's work"—that is, as stemming from evil intent—the conclusion that people do these things because they are mentally disturbed in some way or another usually satisfies our explanatory cravings.

It is undoubtedly true that some lawbreakers do suffer from mental disturbances, as do some nonoffenders. The problem in

* Freudians, however, have sought to attribute stealing to unconscious motivations stemming from deep-seated psychological conflicts or personality disorders. (E.g., Abrahamsen, 1945.)

assessing the validity of psychogenic claims as general explanations of criminality, however, is in determining the extent to which emotional disturbances are causally related to criminal behavior. If, for example, a significantly higher proportion of the criminal population than of the general population suffers from a given mental disorder, it could be argued that this "condition" precipitated the offenders' conduct. However, the studies designed to test psychogenic claims have so far been less than successful.

In a critique of psychiatric theories, Michael Hakeem (1958) points to some of the basic problems surrounding efforts to test causal assertions of this sort. In most cases few differences are found between criminal (or delinquent) and noncriminal populations. Where differences do exist, the validity of the results is often questionable. In any case, factors other than psychological ones correlate more highly with criminal conduct; it may be, therefore, that mental disturbances and criminality are *both* the result of a third set of factors and are not directly related to each other in any significant way.

Probably the greatest single defect of the research on psychogenic theories is the simple fact that the diagnosis of mental illness is itself far from a cut-and-dried procedure. It could very well be that the mental difficulty supposedly causing a person to violate the law is but a formulation of the person's conduct in psychological terminology. Psychoanalysts and psychiatrists usually encounter a law violator after he has been convicted or accused of committing some criminal act. Frequently by the time the individual is even brought to an analyst's attention he has experienced official processing to a considerable extent. It could be that any mental pathology "uncovered" by the analyst is a result of the official processing or occurred as a consequence of the individual's involvement in wrongdoing rather than being the cause of the behavior. Gibbons (1968:165), for example, suggests that

> . . . there is little occasion for surprise when it is discovered that *prison inmates, training school wards* or other examples of *incarcerated* offenders turn out to differ from ostensibly noncriminal or nondelinquent individuals, particularly in terms of hostility, negativism, and antagonism toward authority figures. Observation of negligible differences would be reason for bemusement, for it is unlikely that the experi-

cnce of incarceration has neutral effects upon the self-image and attitudes of prisoners. [Emphasis in original.]

A second difficulty centers on the fact that since the psychiatrist sees the individual after his involvement in criminality, the diagnosis of mental disorder may itself be non-objective. As Schur (1969:68) points out, simply knowing that a person is a convicted or accused murderer, drug addict, delinquent, or whatever may bias the analyst's approach to the subject so that he may "conclude" at the outset that the person is "obviously" disturbed, without fully investigating whether the person is in fact mentally ill. Rather, the emphasis is shifted to the form the assumed disturbance takes or to its underlying causes. Typically, what occurs is that the analyst retrospectively interprets the person's early history and characteristics in such a way as to confirm his preformed conclusion. The person's behavior thus becomes evidence to support what the analyst assumes to exist rather than a phenomenon to be explained.

Finally, there is reason to believe that diagnostic decisions are far from free of cultural or class bias. It may very well be that such factors as membership in a certain ethnic or economic group have much to do with determining whether or not legal authorities accuse a person of violating the law. If the analyst is also influenced by such factors in arriving at a diagnosis, then the person's diagnosed psychopathy, like his perceived criminality, may reflect extraneous factors rather than his mental characteristics.

Some criminally defined people may very well exhibit compulsive, irrational, uncontrollable, and non-goal-oriented personality traits. But many do not. Nor are these traits absent among the larger population of non-offenders. Hence, as a general approach to the explanation of criminal conduct, psychogenic arguments leave much to be desired. In short, the possibility that studies of the relation of mental disorder and criminality reveal more about the biases of the investigators than they do about the characteristics of offenders (Sutherland and Cressey, 1966:170) should be considered seriously when evaluating any claim regarding psychological causes of crime.

Social Conditions In recent years it has become increasingly popular to attribute criminality to the social conditions or life experiences encountered by individuals. Whereas biogenic and psychogenic explanations of criminal behavior attribute this conduct to some peculiarity of the individual criminal, sociogenic theories attempt to locate the causes of crime in the social environments faced by lawbreakers. Biogenic and psychogenic approaches look for causal conditions *within* the individual; sociogenic arguments, on the other hand, turn *outward* to the social forces that shape human conduct. These three perspectives differ in that explanatory emphasis is placed on different types of factors. All three, however, attempt to discover the faulty or abnormal conditions—biochemical, psychological, or social—that supposedly account for the undesirable behavior of individuals. Evil, after all, is the cause of evil. What is more logical than to explain evil by locating the undesirable conditions that give rise to it?

Like the other approaches, sociogenic arguments are many and varied. Most of these theories have to do with crime rates and are not directly concerned with individual etiology; extensive discussion of the major sociological explanations of crime is therefore postponed until Chapter 6. At this point we seek only to indicate the general nature of these theories by illustrating a few of the major contentions.

Sociogenic theories of crime have scrutinized virtually every kind of social factor with any conceivable causal relevance. Most commonly, criminal conduct has been attributed to defects in child-rearing practices (both overpermissiveness and extreme restrictiveness), family environment, or peer-group associates, to poverty and affluence, and to similar factors. The relationship between family life and criminal conduct, for example, has received a good deal of attention in both sociological literature and the popular press.)

Interest in the family as a causal factor rests on rational grounds. The family is known to have an intimate and constant influence on the individual, at least from infancy through adolescence. Family relationships largely shape the individual's values, morality, and, consequently, his behavior. Even in adult life, family influences are assumed to be crucial in directing behavior, so that child-rearing patterns, home-life conditions, interpersonal relationships within the family, and the like could conceivably operate in specific ways to produce criminality.

A wealth of literature exists dealing with this topic. Most of the research has focused on juvenile delinquency, although a few studies have attempted to trace adult criminality to early family experiences. In summarizing the various claims made regarding the family and crime,(Sutherland and Cressey (1966:217) found that six conditions are commonly emphasized as related to criminal conduct. That is, criminality is said to be likely to occur when: (1) other members of the family are criminal, delinquent, or alcoholic; (2) the home has been "broken" by divorce, death, or desertion; (3) parental control is lacking; (4) disruptive or uncongenial family relationships exist, stemming from dominance, jealousy, neglect, favoritism, and the like; (5) the family is marked by unconventional social arrangements, such as racial or religious mixing, or the home atmosphere is somehow abnormal, as in a foster home or an institutional environment; and (6) unemployment and other financial difficulties disrupt the family.

The second condition has been one of the most widely asserted and researched. A number of people have sought to show that delinquency and crime are largely caused by broken home environments.(For example, in a controversial study, Sheldon and Eleanor Glueck (1951) concluded that such defective family patterns are the major causes of delinquency.) Several studies have tended to confirm this conclusion, showing that a higher proportion of delinquent youngsters than of non-delinquents come from broken homes, so that the broken home could be an important source of crime.

But research has shown that other factors seem to be as closely related to delinquency as is family cohesion. It may be, then, that the broken home is but one of a number of variables that act together to generate illegal conduct. Also, most of the studies relating crime to defective family patterns are biased in that they deal largely or exclusively with lower-class gang delinquents. If attention were to shift to other forms of delinquent conduct or to other types of delinquents, such as middle-class offenders, the generalization that broken homes are the major cause of delinquency would probably have to be modified.

Undoubtedly family factors are important influences on certain forms of criminality. But to attribute crime as such to intra-familial relationships or some peculiarity of the home environment is simply a case of overgeneralization. A similar conclusion can be reached regarding all other arguments that seek to attribute criminal conduct to one or another kind of social circumstance.

Differential Association   To many criminologists, Sutherland's theory of differential association (Sutherland and Cressey, 1966: 81–82) represents a major explanatory breakthrough. The mature version of this theory, which first appeared in 1939, represents a substantial break with other general theoretic approaches in that it seeks to "normalize" the criminal. That is, rather than searching for some unusual condition or conditions that somehow cause people to commit crimes, Sutherland sought to attribute criminal conduct to the same types of factors that generate noncriminal behavior. Like other forms of human conduct, criminal activity, Sutherland claimed, is acquired in a process of social interaction. In short, one learns to be a criminal.

In effect, Sutherland proposed, persons will come to engage in criminal conduct when they acquire sentiments in favor of law violation that outweigh anticriminal orientations. This suggests that one can be exposed to both pro- and anti-law-violating moralities. A person comes to adopt criminal as opposed to noncriminal behavior patterns when he learns how to violate laws and when the values conducive to putting that knowledge into practice are stronger than the person's anticriminal sentiments.

The elements of Sutherland's theory are summarized in nine propositions:

1. Criminal behavior is learned.
2. Criminal behavior is learned in interaction with other persons in a process of communication.
3. The principal part of the learning of criminal behavior occurs within intimate personal groups.
4. The learning of criminal behavior includes (a) techniques of committing a crime, which are sometimes very complex, sometimes very simple; and (b) the specific direction of motives, drives, rationalizations, and attitudes.

5. The specific direction of motives, drives, etc. is learned from definitions of the legal codes as favorable or unfavorable.

6. A person becomes delinquent because of an excess of definitions favorable to violation of law over definitions unfavorable to violation of law. (This is the principle of differential association.)

7. Differential association may vary in frequency, duration, priority, and intensity.

8. The process of learning criminal behavior by association with criminal and anticriminal patterns involves all of the mechanisms that are involved in any other learning.

9. Although criminal behavior is an expression of general needs and values, it is not explained by these needs and values, since noncriminal behavior is an expression of the same needs and values.

The significant feature of Sutherland's theory is his claim that procriminal sentiments are acquired, as are all others, by association with other individuals in a process of social interaction. Criminal orientations do not, thus, stem from faulty metabolism, inadequate superego development, or even poverty. Why one person should acquire these orientations and another avoid them is not an issue Sutherland felt compelled to explain within the theory. A number of feasible explanations have been suggested, and some of these will be reviewed later in this chapter. But the significance of Sutherland's theory is not to be faulted by its failure to explain something it did not purport to explain.

The theory, however, is not without its critics. Some have attacked the theory's ambiguity and lack of testability. Other writers have noted that the theory applies only to some forms of criminality but fails to explain the totality of crime. Differential association may very well account for professional theft and similar kinds of conduct, but what about statutory rape and other compulsive types of crime that involve little if any training?

Most of these attacks have been answered by Sutherland's student Donald Cressey (1960). Cressey's evaluation of the differential-association theory in light of these criticisms is probably the most accurate assessment of the theory's merits yet formulated. As Cressey notes, the theory's lack of precision and testability is a serious drawback. But by negating the notion that criminality arises from some simple-minded claim regarding family life, emotional insecurity, physical abnormality, and the like, Sutherland made a valuable and important contribution to the study of criminal etiology.

Several attempts have been made to recast differential-association theory into a more satisfactory form. DeFleur and Quinney (1966), for example, suggest that different forms of differential-association may be linked to various kinds of criminal conduct. A professional thief, for instance, may have had certain "kinds" of learning experiences, different from those underlying the behavior of a youthful joyrider. Hence, where the theory fails to provide a general account of crime, it may serve as a useful framework to explain particular forms of criminality. As we shall see, the idea that criminal behavior is learned in interaction with others does indeed help to explain some forms of conduct. But the theory is less successful when applied to other kinds of criminality.

Conclusion

> The basic problem with theories of criminality is that the forms of conduct included are extremely varied. Consequently, any formulation which purports to explain crime must be more elegant, elaborate, and detailed than any conceptualization now extant. It is not that existing general theories are false. Rather, they are plausible but basically untestable. In addition, they are not sufficiently specific in their claims regarding ways in which particular factors conjoin to produce crime of one kind or another [Gibbons, 1968:188].

To date no general theory has found systematic verification in the research designed to test its claims. Several theories do indeed provide insights into the genesis of some forms of crime. But all fall short of explaining the range of phenomena they purport to explain. At present we simply lack any general approach that adequately explains all forms of criminal behavior.

The principal fallacy of general theories rests on their attempt to encompass an extremely broad and diverse realm of activity within one explanatory framework. In most cases, more forms of criminality fall outside the theory's explanatory powers than are accounted for by its arguments. Conversely, if a theory can be expanded to apply to activities so diverse as burglary, child molesting, joyriding, consumer fraud, and unlawful assembly, it is likely to be so vague as to be useless.

Undoubtedly, the search for "the" cause of crime will continue. If past efforts are any indication, the prognosis as to the outcome of this activity is dismal indeed. Yet, while no single theory may adequately explain all the activities comprising criminal behavior, it could be that each type of crime is caused by a different set of factors. If this is so, criminologists might do better to turn their attention to specific forms of crime, attempting to demonstrate why, for example, people embezzle, embark on a life career of professional thievery, molest children, evade income taxes, or joyride, rather than seeking to account for crime in general.

THEORIES EXPLAINING SPECIFIC FORMS OF CRIME

A number of writers have proposed theories designed to explain specific criminal acts or forms of behavior. Several of these theories represent some of the best work yet to appear in causal inquiry. A few of these are reviewed in this section.

Check Forgery   Check forgery technically occurs when an individual writes a check on a fictitious account, a closed account, or an account containing insufficient funds to cover the value of the check. Although it is fairly common for people to write checks that "bounce," most of this activity is probably unintentional and, unless fraud is involved, is not criminal according to the law. Hence, relatively few of the individuals who "forge" a check are actually subjected to criminal prosecution for check forgery.

In a study of "naïve" check forgery, based on statistical data on 1,023 cases of forgery and intensive interviews with 29 convicted forgers, Edwin Lemert (1953) found that forgers on the whole tend to be noncriminal in orientation, older than other convicts, white males with higher-than-average intelligence ratings and substantial educational backgrounds, and with a history of fairly high-status occupations. Moreover, they have little by way of delinquent or criminal records, so that "it can be stated that forgers come from a class of persons we would ordinarily not expect to yield recruits to the criminal population." Why, then, should they forge checks?

On the basis of his findings, Lemert suggested that this conduct can be attributed to several "situational" factors that impinge on the individual. The majority of the people investigated were immersed in a progressive condition of social isolation; that is, they experienced increasing alienation from conventional social bonds. For example, divorce and separation from the family dominated the case histories. The forgers exhibited a high incidence of other isolating conditions, such as loss of job and physical mobility. In addition, many of the subjects had experienced gambling losses, alcoholic sprees, business failures, and similar problems. According to Lemert, the condition of being socially isolated is a necessary prerequisite for "naïve" check forgery.

But why check forgery? Why not something else? According to Lemert's analysis, the choice of forgery can be explained by the circumstances occurring immediately prior to the act. In most cases the individual had become involved in a course of action to which he was symbolically and emotionally committed and which he felt compelled to bring to completion. For example, the forger might be at the races with friends or associates or involved in a drinking spree. In any case, midway through the encounter the individual found himself short of funds. Now, given the situation of social isolation, the individual might feel it presumptuous to ask his associates for money. Hence, to keep the activity going and to retain his, if only temporary, relationship, forging a check is seen as an immediate solution to the situational tensions of the moment.

Check forgery is selected simply because other alternatives do not present themselves to the individual. Moreover, check forgery is technically and psychologically easy to perform and to justify. No special skills are required to forge a check, and, after all, the person can always make good on the check at some later time. These features of check forgery—the lowered or suspended inhibitions the individual may have had concerning criminal conduct, resulting from his being socially isolated, and the situational demands of the moment—conspire to generate this form of criminality and must be present before naïve check forgery will occur.

Embezzlement In a similar inquiry, Donald Cressey (1953) formulated a theory to explain criminal violations of financial trust, of which embezzlement is one form, based on data obtained from a sample of 133 prisoners who had occupied positions of financial trust but had violated that trust by committing a criminal act. After rejecting several plausible hypotheses regarding this behavior, Cressey arrived at the following conclusion:

> Trusted persons become trust violators when they conceive of themselves as having a financial problem which is nonsharable, are aware that this problem can be secretly resolved by violating the position of financial trust, and are able to apply to their own conduct in that situation verbalizations which enable them to adjust their conceptions of themselves as trusted persons with their conceptions as users of the entrusted funds or property [p. 39].

Cressey did not suggest that trust violation would necessarily follow as a direct result of these factors, but he indicated that this process had to occur before trust violation could take place.

To elaborate, Cressey saw his theory as an example of learning theory insofar as the knowledge of how to violate a position of financial trust must be present prior to the circumstances leading to the act. Obviously people who achieve positions of this sort acquire the necessary skills to violate their positions by the same learning process that is involved in acquiring the knowledge necessary to carry out their jobs in the first place. When one learns how to be an accountant, one also learns how to fake the books. But this does not, of course, explain the choice to embezzle, since many people who possess this same knowledge do not use it in an illegal way.

Cressey identified several situational contingencies prerequisite to putting this illicit knowledge into practice, and he found that, prior to committing the act, the trusted individual has to develop rationalizations and justifications that allow him to violate the law. In most cases, the trust violator felt that he was causing no real harm because he intended to replace the money all along. Although large sums may have accumulated over time, the amounts taken at any one time were usually insignificant, so that the person felt no irreparable loss would result. But what sparked the formation of these kinds of rationalizations?

Cressey found that the large majority of trust violators were in financial difficulties, usually related to status aspirations. These difficulties were felt by the individual to be unsharable and capable of being resolved only by financial means. For example, a bank or corporate accountant may gamble in an attempt to emulate a style of life far beyond his financial capacity; he may experience severe losses from this illicit conduct, which, if known to others, would damage his reputation and social standing. Hence, the person felt that the economic problem arising from this behavior had to be resolved in secret. Because "borrowing a little money from the firm" would solve the problem without anyone's being the wiser, embezzlement or some similar form of trust violation was selected as a means of solving a personally important and pressing problem.

Like Lemert's analysis, Cressey's formulation stands as a classic example of "situational" explanations of criminal conduct. In contrast to Sutherland's "genetic" approach, which sought to locate the factors occurring in the early life history of a person that lead him to violate the law, the situational approach emphasizes processes occurring at or near the time the person committed some criminal act. It may be that a situational approach is best applied to trust violation and check forgery, but these forms of misconduct do not exhaust the list. Perhaps other types of wrongdoing can be accounted for by a genetic explanation. The various attempts to explain gang delinquency illustrate the applicability of these alternative models.

Gang Delinquency An impressive body of literature has accumulated regarding the behavior of lower-class gang delinquents. Stimulated by Albert Cohen's contentions regarding the causes of working-class delinquent behavior, a number of theories —largely in opposition to Cohen's—have been put forward to explain this form of criminality.

In his book *Delinquent Boys* (1955), Cohen argued that the origins of gang delinquency are to be found in a basic structural defect of American society, where working-class boys are placed in situations incompatible with their abilities. In school and elsewhere, working-class boys are largely evaluated by and expected to live up to middle-class standards. Since working-class boys lack the socialization and environmental prerequisites to meet the criteria of their middle-class evaluators, they are not able to compete with their more affluent peers. Hence they often experience severe status anxieties and assaults on their self-esteem. As a result, working-class boys tend to withdraw from these stress-producing situations and seek consolation among others who share similar problems of status and rejection. Within this group the youngsters find standards and opportunities to resolve their status difficulties by establishing criteria of performance compatible with their cultural experiences. In large part, these values and behavioral standards are in contradiction to and directly conflict with the ones espoused by middle-class society. In this sense, the antisocial behavior of lower-class gang delinquents can be understood as a form of rebellion against middle-class morality, a rebellion generated by the basic incompatibility of a middle-class style of life with lower-class social and cultural experiences.

Cohen suggests that much of the delinquent behavior of lower-class gang members, for instance, involves nonutilitarian, malicious, negativistic forms of conduct. Lower-class boys steal, but not for money. Rather, they steal "for the hell of it." Theft is thus one way of expressing their rebellion, not only by flaunting middle-class laws but also by showing their disdain for the acquisitive values of the middle-class. Through this nonutilitarian behavior, gang members acquire a reputation, status, and a sense of belonging to a group that shares their despair.

In opposition to Cohen, Richard Cloward and Lloyd Ohlin (1960) suggest that gang delinquency does not stem from the failure to live up to middle-class standards but, rather, is generated by a disjunction between the goals sought by lower-class youths and the means available to them to achieve these aspirations. Although lower-class members apparently do not aspire to a middle-class style of life, they have internalized an emphasis on conventional goals of success and material affluence. Since they are unable to achieve these aspirations by legitimate (middle-class) methods, pressure builds up to engage in illegitimate behavior as alternative means. For example, lacking the opportunity to go to college and acquire a respectable and well-paid professional career, some lower-class youngsters turn to burglary as a way of acquiring the sought-after dollar. It is not their rejection of middle-class values that leads lower-class youths to crime. Quite the reverse. They engage in criminality precisely because they aspire to values they have no legitimate means to attain.

The particular form of criminality that is adopted depends, Cloward and Ohlin suggest, largely on the cultural milieu in which a person finds himself. For example, in neighborhoods where crime is well organized and rooted, a "criminalistic" gang subculture is likely to develop in which theft and similar forms of conduct will predominate. In other areas conflict or "bobbing" gangs will emerge.

Another alternative to Cohen's thesis is offered by Walter Miller (1958), who set forth certain notions regarding the "focal concerns" or cultural values of lower-class society. Miller argued that certain structural peculiarities of lower-class society, notably the female-dominated household resulting from the practice of "serial monogamy" (a custom wherein women experience a succession of mates but no permanent husband), lead to sex-role identification problems for lower-class boys. With no permanent role model in the household for the boys to emulate, at a relatively young age they turn to their peer group for a social environment in which to confirm and display their maleness. This structural situation, coupled with the focal concerns of lower-class boys (which Miller identifies as toughness, trouble, smartness, excitement, fate, autonomy), produces various forms of criminality common to lower-class groups. For example, lower-class boys display their toughness by fighting, achieve excitement by robbing the corner candy store, and demonstrate smartness by outwitting the police.

Illegal or immoral conduct, like gang fighting, joyriding, rape, and theft, are, Miller suggests, culturally available means of attaining goals that are characteristic of lower-class society. Gang delinquency, in this view, does not represent either a rejection of middle-class goals or a lack of opportunity to achieve them. Rather, the behavioral patterns of lower-class delinquents are related to their differences from middle-class society in both culturally meaningful goals and culturally available means to achieve those goals. It is these cultural differences between. the lower class and the middle class that are responsible for gang delinquency, not some malady of the social structure as such.

These three theories are alike in implying that delinquent

conduct stems from positive motivations to violate legal codes. Whether the motivation is an attempt to rebel against society, to achieve what society has denied them, or to pursue an entirely different set of values, lower-class juveniles are, according to these arguments, propelled to commit illegal acts by social pressures. Presumably they would not so behave were the situation otherwise.

Whereas Cohen, Cloward and Ohlin, and Miller postulate a more or less genetic explanation of gang delinquency, a situational model may actually be more appropriate insofar as the factors said to cause this conduct stem from conditions lying deep in the offender's past which operate to motivate him to violate the law. For example, David Matza (1964) found that no particularly strong motivations operate to force gang members to behave in illegal ways. Rather, delinquents tend to "drift" into this kind of behavior as a "normal" part of a life career in lower-class settings. Although lower-class boys generally adhere to societal standards of appropriate conduct, various rationalizations and situational conditions allow them to relax their moral constraints and to exonerate themselves from blame for committing illegal acts. But nothing forces them to break the law. Delinquent activities, that is, seem to be "situational" in character, arising from the circumstances of the moment.

It has also been suggested that even this theory misses the point. Delinquents, it is argued, do not have to be motivated to violate moral codes; nor is it necessary that they dull their inhibitions against deviating behavior by rationalizing their conduct—because they largely do not subscribe to the codes they violate in the first place (Hindelang, 1970). It may be that lower-class gang delinquents subscribe to a cultural morality quite different from that of middle-class society. If this is the case, there is little reason for them to feel obliged to adhere to middle-class codes of conduct. Whereas the middle-class accountant may find mugging an inexcusable act of aggression, a lower-class gang delinquent may harbor no such definition. Mugging, after all, can be profitable. For the lower-class gang delinquent, not adhering to the moral constraints of the middle class, the question may be more a matter of "Why not?" than "Why?"

The research dealing with gang delinquency is so far inconclusive regarding the various explanations that purport to account for this behavior. Probably both situational and genetic factors are involved in the genesis of the illegal behavior. For other forms of criminal behavior, however, a strictly genetic model seems to serve best. This is especially the case for professional theft.

Professional Theft The professional thief probably corresponds more closely than does any other lawbreaker to the common stereotype of the hardened criminal. The con-artist, pickpocket, shop-lifter, and burglar who steal professionally have been objects of fascination and debate among criminologists for generations. Much research has been devoted to professional theft, so that descriptions of professional thievery and theories seeking to explain this conduct abound. Most of this material is descriptive in character. Thus, a good deal is known about the activities pursued by professional thieves. But relatively little information is available regarding the factors causing individuals to take up theft as a way of life.

The seminal statement on professional theft is found in Sutherland's book *The Professional Thief* (1937). It was in the course of his study of professional thieves that Sutherland generated his general theory of differential association. Although Sutherland provides little insight into why people become professional thieves (he did, however, suggest that some kind of crisis situation usually provided the stimulus), his description of what is involved in adopting theft as a way of life is revealing and may have a wide range of applicability.

According to Sutherland (1937:211) the "absolutely necessary, universal, and definitive characteristic of the professional thief" is *recognition* by other members of the profession. In order to be a professional thief and to engage in stealing as a full-time practitioner, one has to be "initiated" into the "fraternity." In order for this to occur, the person must be selected by other professional thieves and tutored in the arts of the trade. *Selection* and *tutelage*, then, "are the universal factors in an explanation of the genesis of the professional thief. A person cannot acquire recognition as a professional thief until he has had tutelage in professional theft, and tutelage is given only to a few persons selected from the total population."

In short, in order to enter the profession of theft, or any other profession, a person has to undergo training. This training involves not only development of the techniques and skills required to steal successfully. It also instills a philosophy of life that serves to nullify any inhibitions the neophyte may have regarding his activity. Moreover, in the course of becoming a full-fledged member of the profession, one also learns how to relate to other thieves, to avoid apprehension, and to deal with the law in case of arrest. All of this, of course, takes time and an ongoing association with others who share this way of life. Whatever may motivate a person to be a professional thief is of relative insignificance compared to the conditions that Sutherland indicates as essential to admission into the "clan." Many people probably have an inclination to steal, but few ever have an opportunity to fulfill that desire on a full-time basis. The motivation to steal is not enough to explain professional theft.

The research regarding this type of criminality tends to be of an autobiographical, case-history variety. The majority of this research supports Sutherland's claims, although there is some dispute as to the professional standing of some full-time thieves, or "grifters," as they call themselves. The few cases that contradict some of Sutherland's specific points may reflect methodological peculiarities of case-history research. For example, if one individual indicates that he had no contact with other professional thieves in the course of his career whereas another person complies with Sutherland's requirements, it is difficult to determine which is the negative or "deviant" case. Sutherland's theory applies to a particular form or variety of career criminality, so that research which seems to contradict some of his claims may actually be dealing with a different kind of criminality.

Conclusion The theories reviewed in this section represent a small fraction of the accounts available in the literature. Regardless of the particular merits of any of these analyses, theories of specific types of crime are significant because they offer an alternative to those with grand theoretical claims. At least theories of a more limited scope are testable, so that the accuracy of their claims can be assessed with a reasonable degree of precision. Criminologists can probably learn more about the causes of criminal conduct by focusing on a few intelligently chosen cases than from all the sweeping generalizations of the grand-theory approach. It may very well be that a number of factors conjoin in specific ways to produce various types of criminal conduct.

But we are faced with a problem: No end is in sight as to the number of theories it will take to explain the phenomena addressed. Particularistic theories can be spun *ad infinitum* with little general theoretical growth. What is needed is some model, as opposed to a general theory of criminality, that can embrace a variety of factors within a single set of concepts and explanatory propositions and that could, therefore, serve as a basis for explaining a variety of forms of criminality. Efforts to this end are found in a number of the typologies of crime that have recently appeared. The following section reviews several examples of this approach.

THE TYPOLOGICAL APPROACH

In recent years it has become clear to many criminologists that no single theory can adequately explain the numerous and diverse forms of criminal behavior. Nor does the proliferation of particularistic theories of forms of criminality hold much promise, since a theory that adequately accounts for one form of criminal conduct may not apply to others. Yet, even though crime does indeed consist of heterogeneous forms of activity, it is conceivable that these various forms of behavior can be classified into more or less homogeneous groupings or types. Different factors may operate so as to generate the various forms. By organizing these varied patterns of behavior within a typological framework, it would then be possible to identify the various kinds of factors that generate specific types of criminality. For example, while peer-group associations may be significant in generating certain kinds of criminal behavior, differential association does not apply to all types of crime, and different kinds of association may underlie different forms of criminality. A well-constructed typology could be helpful in sorting out those cases for which this variable has explanatory relevance.

A number of attempts have been made to construct typologies

of crime. Unfortunately, this approach has not advanced much beyond a vague and often ambiguous statement to the effect that a number of types of crime exist, whereupon several examples are listed. The system employed to construct these types is either absent or poorly identified. Or the characteristics used to define the various types are conspicuously missing. Moreover, there has been little research to test the various schemas advanced, so that judgments as to the inclusiveness or validity of these taxonomies are at best speculative. However, the inadequacies of typological efforts that are apparent so far should not lead one to overlook the potential of this approach. A brief overview of several typologies may provide some indication of the nature and extent of typological efforts.

Typologies of Delinquents   In a study of 15 typologies dealing with juvenile delinquency, John Kinch (1962) demonstrated that most writers were actually describing three major types of delinquents. Kinch's report noted that these 15 schemas shared at least one definitional factor: All emphasized the group orientation of the youngsters as a major classificatory variable. Kinch contended that, on the basis of this attribute, existing typologies have been systematically identifying "prosocial," "antisocial," and "asocial" delinquents. It is possible, therefore, that the various investigations surveyed are, in fact, dealing with real delinquent types. For example, delinquents with prosocial attitudes may exhibit basically similar patterns of behavior that are fundamentally different from the behavioral patterns typical of asocial or antisocial delinquents. Moreover, as Kinch concluded, it may be that "reference group" is an important defining variable for constructing delinquent types.

A second study by Kinch (1962a) classified a group of delinquents in terms of the three types he had identified. Once the youngsters were classified, Kinch ascertained the variations in self-images held by the boys comprising each type. The "prosocial" delinquents indicated that they conceived of themselves in a conventional, socially acceptable way. The "antisocial" delinquents saw themselves in a less favorable light. And the "asocial" delinquents described themselves as confused and nervous and seemed to be well aware of their "rejected" status.

This research suggests that delinquents characteristically differ in terms of their social orientations and self-orientations and that variations in these attitudes are related to different patterns of delinquent behavior. But, then, nondelinquents probably show variations in these attributes as well.

Psychiatrist Richard Jenkins had previously (1944) identified three types of delinquents analogous to those described by Kinch. Jenkins postulated a group that he called "unsocialized aggressive" delinquents, which resembles Kinch's "asocial" type. This group is characterized by a pervasive pattern of severe parental rejection. Jenkins also pointed to a group of "socialized" or "pseudo-socialized" delinquents and a small group of "emotionally disturbed" delinquents which also exhibit some similarity to the types Kinch describes.

A third example of delinquent typologies is represented by the I-level (Interpersonal Maturity Level) schema currently employed by the California Youth Authority in its Community Treatment Program for delinquents. This typology is based on the theory of Sullivan, Grant, and Grant (1957), which postulates seven successive stages of growth in "interpersonal maturity." These levels of development range from level one, "least mature"—a level that apparently represents a social moron—to the ideal of social maturity, level seven, which few people ever achieve. The individual is classified within this system according to his perceptions of himself and the world. According to the officials using the system, delinquents generally fall into maturity levels two through five, although very few ever make it to level five. Within each level, subtypes of delinquents have been identified, resulting in nine subtypes in all. These subtypes include a full range of emotional and social attitudes from "asocial, aggressive," to "cultural conformist," to "culture identifiers."

Typologies of Criminals Although fewer in number than delinquent typologies, several efforts have been made to construct typologies of adult offenders. One of these taxonomies was developed by Julian Roebuck (1966), based largely on legal categories of offense behavior. Roebuck developed his typology by inductive analysis of the over-all criminal careers of 1,155 prison inmates. The convicts were categorized according to their criminal-arrest (or "rap sheet") records. By this technique, thirteen types were identified, including the "jack-of-all-trades" offender, the "single pattern of robbery" offender, the "double pattern of larceny and burglary" offender, and the like. Although Roebuck's typology has some merit in that he analyzed criminal careers longitudinally, it is doubtful that legal categories provide an adequate base on which to develop typologies of offenders. Nor is a sample of convicted felons reliable for constructing a typology purporting to encompass the totality of criminal types.

Other offender typologies have been suggested by Ruth Cavan (1955) and Herbert Bloch and Gilbert Geis (1962). Cavan based her typology on the degree of the person's withdrawal or exclusion from control by the dominant social organization. In these terms, Cavan identified five basic types of offender and several subtypes. Although she illustrated each type in a case-history fashion, Cavan neglected to stipulate the criteria used to classify offenders. The same problem plagues the typology offered by Bloch and Geis. Their classification includes "organized crime," "white-collar crime," and "sex offenses." Typologies of this sort are inadequate for explanatory purposes, nor is it likely that these typologies will be of much value in identifying lawbreakers.

A similar conclusion can be drawn regarding some of the more recent typological efforts. Daniel Glaser's (1972) typology of offender types, for example, bears unique labels—e.g., "adolescent recapitulators," "subcultural assaultants," "crisis-vacillation predators," and others. An alternative typology has been formulated by Clinard and Quinney (1967). This appears to be a classification of behavior rather than of criminals, and it is not clear which purpose the taxonomy was designed to serve. On the basis of the concept of "behavioral systems," Clinard and Quinney identified eight specific types of conduct. To locate a case within a particular type, four identifying characteristics were used: the criminal career of the offender, the extent of group support for his behavior, the correspondence between criminal behavior and legitimate behavior patterns, and societal reaction. The list of types included "political crime," "conventional crime," "public order crime," and other forms of misconduct. Even though

Clinard and Quinney went to some length to delineate and differentiate the various types, the typology suffers from a general ambiguity. How, for example, is one to measure the extent of group support or the correspondence between criminal and legitimate behavioral patterns? The intended meaning of these factors is obvious, but the method by which they may be used to categorize particular cases is less than clear.

Gibbons's Role-Career Approach: One of the more elaborate typological formulations has been offered by Don Gibbons (1968, 1965). This typology departs from other taxonomies in several important ways. For one, it is based on a general theoretical foundation. Second, insofar as the typology is designed for both explanatory and treatment purposes, Gibbons detailed the dimensions involved in categorizing offenders into various types and the background or causal factors important in generating these various types.

The theoretical premise underlying Gibbons's taxonomy is the assumption that criminal behavior can be analyzed as a pattern of *social roles*. The category "criminal" is basically a social status that is attached to corresponding roles or patterns of behavior. People are judged and thereby come to occupy one or another criminal status in terms of the kinds of criminality they engage in. In short, to be a criminal is to occupy a socially designated position. (This is not, of course, to suggest that the status "criminal" is descriptive of the person in totality. "Criminal" is but one of the many statuses a person may occupy, although all his other statuses may be affected by his identity as a criminal.)

What is significant here is that not all criminal statuses are identical, except in terms of their outcast character, so that occupants of different criminal statuses (e.g., child molester compared to burglar) exhibit different patterns of offenses or role-related behavior. Differences in offense behavior, then, are a principal variable for differentiating offenders into distinct behavioral or role types.

Second, statuses are determined essentially by the role expectations of others. Some criminal conduct is carried out in isolation whereas other forms typically take place in a group setting. In sorting offenders into role types, the social circumstances surrounding an individual's criminality become a principal definitional dimension.

Third, the incumbents of specific social statuses tend to hold similar role conceptions or self-image patterns and role-related attitudes. Since a person's conception of himself is likely to influence his behavior, self-image and general societal attitudes provide another dimension for constructing distinct types.

Fourth, role behavior tends to vary in duration and complexity. Some individuals experience long and varied criminal careers extending throughout their lives, whereas others concentrate on a specific form of criminal conduct. Still others violate the law once and never repeat the same or any other crime. Thus, criminal types can be further distinguished on the basis of the role career or offender patterns exhibited by various individuals. In this way the person who is apprehended for cashing a phony check once differs from the individual who makes a business of check forging.

On the basis of these factors, Gibbons designated the following definitional dimensions as important in categorizing criminals: the person's offense behavior, the interactional setting, the self-conception and attitudes held by the offender, and his role career.

So far Gibbons has been able to identify nine delinquent types and 21 adult offender types. A few examples of each may suggest the comprehensiveness of the typology. Included are the "conflict-gang delinquent," the "automobile thief-joyrider," the "overly aggressive delinquent," and the "behavioral-problem delinquent." The adult typology includes the "professional thief," the "amateur shoplifter," the "embezzler," the "psychopathic assaultist," the "male homosexual," the "opiate addict," and the " 'Skid Road' alcoholic."

Assuming that these in fact correspond to real-life offenders, it is likely that different factors operate to generate the various types. As we saw in the review of specific theories, conflict-gang delinquency is not likely to stem from the same factors generating naïve check forgery or professional theft. However, it is also likely that certain kinds of factors conjoin in various ways to produce these offender types. Gibbons suggests that variations in social class, family background, peer-group associates, and the nature of the contact one has with defining agents lead to different offense patterns.

Some criminals are recruited from all social classes, while others originate only from particular classes. Peer-group associates appear to be important in explaining some forms of criminality but are of negligible consequences as far as other kinds of behavior are concerned. Also, various kinds of offenders tend to receive differential treatment by law-enforcement agencies. It is conceivable that the way a person is handled by the police and the courts affects his future behavior so that variations in the kind of experience people have with these authorities could lead to different career patterns. Finally, since self-conceptions, attitudes, basic role orientations, and role-playing skills are acquired largely in family settings, differences in family background may explain some kinds of criminality but not others.

By putting these factors together, a general theoretical model can be generated to account for a wide range of criminal behavior. Although each type is to be explained by a different conjunction of factors, the typology provides an explanatory framework for generating causal claims. Similarly, if different causal conditions relate to different offender types, it may be possible to type the populations of offenders in prison and on probation and to establish different treatment tactics appropriate for the members of each type. In this way the typology could have pragmatic as well as scientific value.

Conclusion Efforts to construct etiological or diagnostic typologies of criminals hold a good deal of appeal for several reasons. If successful, systems for classifying criminals into types could provide a solution to the explanatory difficulties of general and specific theories of criminality. They also provide an alternative to the ad hoc kinds of treatment often received by convicted offenders. So far, however, the typological approach has met with a number of problems, having to do with the degree to which existing typologies fulfill taxonomic requirements, their validity (the degree to which they correspond with reality), and their scientific and pragmatic value.

In an early essay, Gibbons and Garrity (1959) specified the

minimal criteria a typology must meet to be deemed adequate. First, a typology must possess *clarity* and *objectivity*. Second, the types identified must be *mutually exclusive* so that actual cases fit one and only one of the types listed. Third, a typology must be *comprehensive* so that all or most offenders can be placed in one or another of the types identified. Fourth, a typology should be *parsimonious* enough to be usable. As we have seen, most of the typologies currently available are defective as far as one or more of these criteria are concerned.

It is difficult to assess the validity of existing typologies since research directed to testing them is conspicuously absent. In most cases, it would be impossible to test these typologies. There is reason to believe, however, that few if any of the existing tax-onomies have any correspondence to reality. For example, in one study designed to test Gibbons's role-career typology (Hartjen and Gibbons, 1969) it was found that fewer than half of the offenders sampled could be placed in one or another of the types listed by Gibbons. (The study, however, did demonstrate that the typology had some diagnostic potential, since the probation officers en-gaged in the research were able to achieve a high degree of agree-ment as to the "type" or "no-type" status of individual cases.) If more sophisticated classification procedures were employed in the research it is likely that even fewer cases would have been suc-cessfully classified.

A third point is related to this issue. Most of the current typol-ogies overemphasize the dramatic but infrequently encountered forms of criminality. Certainly any typology should include pro-fessional thieves, murderers, embezzlers, rapists, and the like since these crimes tend to generate most of the loss and public concern resulting from crime. But the great bulk of criminality consists of relatively mild nuisance or "folk" kinds of misconduct. Indeed, the largest single category of arrests is for drunkenness, whereas forcible rape constitutes a very small proportion of re-ported crime. A typology that fails to include these garden-variety forms of criminality is of little value for either explanatory or treatment purposes since it excludes the majority of phenomena with which it is concerned. Moreover, typologies that emphasize the flamboyant forms of criminality not only foster a stereotyped image of crime and criminals but also perpetrate a misconception of the phenomena which negates their scientific usefulness (see Hartjen and Gibbons, 1969).

EXPLANATIONS OF CRIME: A CRITIQUE

The theories discussed in this chapter represent but a few of the various explanations offered to answer, "Why do people break the law?" It is clear from this review that existing theories leave a good deal to be desired. It may well be that criminologists have been asking the wrong question all along. As Bruce Jackson recently commented (1972:26):

> The word *criminal* identifies not a specific kind or style of behavior but rather the way certain actions and kinds of actions are formally evaluated in a particular culture at a particular time. *Crime* is not so much a physical fact as it is a relationship, one that signalizes an attitude. The label of *criminal* is affixed to the actor because of his *presumed* mental set and not because he acted in a certain way.

An act can have different meanings independent of the qualities or characteristics of the behavior. Killing, for example, need not always be an instance of murder. Before killing can be transformed into an act of murder, some assessment of the defendant's mental state must be made. Not only does a person have to be legally sane before guilt can be ascribed, it is also necessary that he be shown as having intended or wished to commit the forbidden act (McHugh, 1970) in order for killing to be conceived as an instance of murder. This requires that some judgment be rendered as to the fundamental moral makeup of the accused. The legal reality of crime is found in the moral assessments legal authorities make of defendants. Whether or not a person will acquire the social status "criminal" does not, therefore, depend solely on his behavior.

In addition to the various problems specific to particular explanatory approaches or theories that were identified above, all etiological efforts share a fundamental flaw more basic than issues of testability or validity. *All theories of criminal behavior rest on an explicit or implicit conception of the world and the nature of man.*

Regardless of the approach, the question of etiology presupposes that "crime" and "criminal" be placed in a common conceptual package. Crime has usually been studied by investigating the behavior or characteristics of persons officially convicted of criminal conduct. But the action to be explained is obscured by equating it with the actors studied. Theories of criminal conduct relating to this inquiry are, therefore, merely encoded descriptions of a "type-of-person" (Hartjen, 1972). Crime has been *objectified* in terms of the characteristics of persons labeled criminals. In essence, crime has been treated as a feature or characteristic of these persons. That is, *crime is described as a function of whatever it is that criminally defined persons do.*

The result of this conceptual confusion has been that, in order to explain crime, it has become necessary to construct some version of this "criminal" type-of-person. Generally this is done by describing the person's biological makeup, goal orientations, family background, emotional state, or whatever. The issue is not whether or not the resulting image is valid. Addiction, for example, may indeed drive some people into violent forms of crime to support their habit. The drug addict-mugger represents one version of a "type-of-person" created by theorists to explain one kind of reality experience. Could crime of any type be conceived without constructing some image of a criminal type of actor? If not, what we "know" about the "causes" of crime is, in the end, but a reflection of the type-of-person created by the theorist in the process of explaining it.

But people do not exist as types. Their *typical* features are ascribed to them by others. Ego is perceived as an instance of a category (social type) because of theoretic (conceptual) formulations others create about him (Holzner, 1968). That is, other people look the way they do because they are perceived in certain ways. Hence, the criminal as a type-of-person is but an artifact of a theoretic formulation.

Now, in so far as the conceptual possibility of crime is located in and is a product of the theorist's description of the criminal as a type-of-person, crime itself is something *created* by the theorist in the process of constructing this type-of-person. If, as we have said, crime is not an instance of reality but a version of one possible conception or image men have of reality, constructing a theory (set of utterances) that purports to explain the existence of crime is one of the *ways* in which this conception of reality is created. In this sense, causal theories of criminal behavior are

CHARLIE CLICHE RIDES AGAIN!

empirically available exemplifications of a reality conception. It is not that these theories are necessarily false. The issue of validity is irrelevant here. Rather, theories of crime can be treated as data and studied in their own right, not for what they tell us about criminal behavior, but for what they tell us about how the conception of crime is created—for what they have to say about how man conceives his world.

In short, instead of asking why people break the law, the focus of criminology should be on how society's members conceive of something called a lawbreaker, and how this conception is realized in practice by attaching this designation to some person. The following chapters of this book address the latter part of this issue.

4

Being Busted: The Police

CRIMINAL LAW AND BEHAVIOR that violates the law can be taken as preconditions for crime. Crime can be said to exist when and if some person's behavior is interpreted as criminal by others. As we have suggested, behavior is not automatically criminalized simply because it violates some criminal code. A person acquires the social designation "criminal" when (and only when) others treat him as a lawbreaker. Formally, this can be said to occur when the law has been applied to the individual accused of crime—that is, when he has been apprehended, prosecuted, and duly pronounced guilty by agents of the law. *The process that results in the application of a criminal identity to some person we have called the criminalization process.* Sociologically, this process can be described and analyzed as a set of actions, which consist of arrest, prosecution, conviction, and punishment.*

In order for someone's behavior to be criminalized, it is first necessary that the person be "identified" (socially recognized) as a "criminal type-of-person." The first official step in accomplishing identification is formal arrest. To describe how an instance of

* Obviously not all individuals accused of breaking the law (i.e., arrested and prosecuted) are adjudicated as guilty. Those who are acquitted of criminal charges are, in a sense, granted a reprieve from a criminal identity.

behavior is transformed into a criminal act, it is necessary that we give some accounting of how arrests are made. That is, under what conditions will this step in the process be initiated? To answer this question, we will focus our attention in this chapter on police behavior and the conditions underlying police decision-making.

POLICE WORK AND ORGANIZATION

In 1971 there were approximately 480,000 police personnel in the United States.* These individuals were employed in over 40,000 separate law-enforcement agencies, with the vast majority assigned to local police departments. Annually about $3 billion is spent on the police. On the average, there were in 1971 about 2.4 police officers per every 1,000 people in the U.S. Large cities tend to have a higher ratio, averaging 3.3 officers per every 1,000 citizens. Suburban areas, on the other hand, average about 1.8 officers for every 1,000 residents.

These 480,000 police officers made an estimated 8,639,700 formal arrests in 1971. Roughly one fourth of these arrests were formally charged and tried, and about 75 per cent of those charged were convicted. This means that on the average each police officer makes 18 arrests of all kinds per year. Given that about one fourth of these persons are actually prosecuted and 75 per cent of these are convicted, we can conclude that about three people per officer per year are convicted of a crime. But these figures are for all types of crimes. In 1971, about 5,995,211 serious crimes† were reported to the police for which 1,707,600 arrests were made. Hence, fewer than 30 per cent of all reported serious crimes were cleared by an arrest. This averages out to approximately four arrests per officer per year for serious crimes. To put it another way, it costs the American taxpayer about $2,000 to arrest someone for a serious crime. Of course, it costs much more than that to convict him.

The picture that emerges from these figures is that police

---

* Unless otherwise indicated, all statistics in this chapter are from the Federal Bureau of Investigation (1971).

† In this chapter serious crimes are defined as those crimes included in the FBI's index of crime—namely, murder, forcible rape, aggravated assault, robbery, burglary, larceny ($50 or more), and automobile theft.

officers are not particularly effective in apprehending the violators of criminal law. This conclusion, however, is somewhat distorted because only a small fraction of police personnel are directly involved in serious law-enforcement work. And very little actual police activity has any direct concern with catching criminals. This is important because the image of the police officer as a law-enforcement officer colors not only the citizen's but also the police officer's conception of "real" police work. Hence, even though most police activities have little to do directly with enforcing the criminal code by detecting and apprehending those suspected of illegal conduct, the image of the policeman as a law-enforcement officer comes to exercise a significant influence on police work-aday behavior.

In recent years a number of studies have appeared regarding the police. Most of this material is descriptive in nature, so that whereas a good deal is known about what the police do in ordinary situations, criminologists do not completely agree as to the conditions generating this behavior. From available evidence, however, it appears that police arrest practices are related to at least three factors: the police function (i.e., the role they are expected to fulfill in society), the organizational and bureaucratic structure of police work, and the working cop's efforts to mediate the inconsistent and often conflicting demands placed on him in carrying out his role. Together, these factors operate to condition the nature and influence the results of police work.

Although it has been glamorized in the mass media, the job of the police officer is best captured in the phrase, "Damned if you do and damned if you don't." By this I mean that the occupational role of police officer is basically conflictual (Hartjen, 1972a: 63-66) in that the police are faced with paradoxical work-role expectations; the fulfillment of their primary function is negated by the requirement that they complete a number of secondary (but no less demanding) tasks. This basic problem of police work is exemplified by the distinction between the tasks of law enforcing and peacekeeping. Officially, the police exist primarily to enforce criminal laws by detecting and apprehending all persons who violate the criminal code. However, as Bittner (1967) points out, historically and typically law enforcement has been only one of the functions performed by the police, even though it is the primary one. Besides enforcing the criminal code, the police are required to maintain the public peace (e.g., by keeping the neighborhood quiet, forestalling conflict, maintaining orderly activities, etc.). Hence, the role of police officer is actually a dual role, that of law officer and that of peace officer.

The law-enforcement function of the police is relatively clear: The police are to uphold the criminal code by arresting (or attempting to arrest) all those who violate the statutes. The function of peacekeeping, however, is less clear and largely undefined. Bittner (1967:699) suggests that peacekeeping comprises all occupational tasks performed by the police that are not directly related to making arrests. In a general sense, peacekeeping activities involve all those circumstances in which procedures not governed by external control or evaluation (as is the case with the decision to arrest) are employed by the police to manage routine situations. Telling a group of juveniles to "move along"; sending an intoxicated person home in a cab "for his own protection"; "checking up" on a homosexual bar; subjecting a "rowdy" looking group of young "toughs" to a body search; and similar activities, while within the ordinary realm of proper police behavior, can best be classified as peace-keeping as opposed to law-enforcement duties. Peacekeeping is directed more toward controlling potential events or preserving orderly routine than to apprehending violators of criminal laws.

The problem, however, is that these two basic police functions, while related and difficult to distinguish empirically, are not necessarily compatible, so that the police, in serving their peace-keeping function, frequently find it necessary to violate their principal mandate of enforcing the law. Moreover, the legal means to carry out police work apply only to law enforcement and not to peace-keeping activities. This is further complicated by the fact that, even though peacekeeping constitutes the bulk of actual police work, both the public and the police view real police activity as basically concerned with enforcing the criminal law (Wilson, 1968:69). As a result, intervention is largely biased in terms of its law-enforcement features so that even ordinary nuisance or peacekeeping events come to be treated by the police as serious matters of law enforcement.

If it is difficult to distinguish conceptually between law-enforcement and peacekeeping functions, it is even more difficult for the police to separate the two in practice. In part, this explains the particular occupational problem faced by the police in routine police work. Frequently, police use extralegal means as well as legal ones when dealing with a specific situation, or they may use formal (legal) procedures (e.g., arrest) in order to handle a situation when extralegal means fail. For example, a "tipsy" hobo may be arrested and criminally charged because he wandered into a respectable neighborhood, refused to "move along" when ordered to do so by the police, and caused a "scene" by loudly insulting the police when confronted. From the perspective of the police, not only is an arrest essential in this case, but few other options are available to the police in handling the situation. In short, the relatively mild disruption caused by the hobo is treated by the police as a problem of law enforcement. While the hobo's behavior may in fact be in violation of the law (i.e., drunk and disorderly), the problem he presents for the police is one of maintaining order (i.e., ensuring the "respectable" appearance of the neighborhood). Extralegal means, like telling the hobo to move along, usually suffice to take care of the problem. But should this tactic fail, in order to carry out their objective, the police can ultimately fall back on their power as law-enforcement agents and treat the case as a matter requiring the application of their power to arrest.

Both occupational roles of the police officer are carried out in an organizational and situational context and are ultimately influenced by structural and situational factors. The organizational structure of police departments is probably of primary importance in influencing at least the style of police work found in a community. How peacekeeping events are to be handled, what crimes are to be investigated, what neighborhoods are to be vigorously patrolled, and the like are largely determined by the organizational considerations of specific police departments. We can, therefore, expect to find a good deal of variation in both law-enforcement policy and operational practices as police departments differ in structure. Moreover, in large departments with highly specialized divisions, we can expect to encounter variations in individual police work depending on an officer's placement in the organizational structure (Bordua and Reiss, 1966).

Most police departments today are large bureaucratic organizations operated in quasi-military fashion. Officers and patrolmen are enmeshed in a system of subordination along operational and locational lines. Although all units of a particular department may be related to a central command (usually the commissioner), the over-all chain of command is divided into units, so that different precincts or squads are immediately responsible to a localized authority. As yet it is not clear just how the social organization of police departments affects police behavior in the field. The influence is probably greater than is presently thought to be the case. Undoubtedly, the immediate supervisors (precinct captains and sergeants) wield some power over beat cops, but the extent to which they can determine the behavior of their subordinates has not as yet been fully investigated.

We do know, however, that the functional division of police departments along activity lines leads to different "styles" of law enforcement in the field. For example, enforcing narcotic drug laws involves a different kind of procedural activity than pounding a beat on Skid Row.* Whereas the Skid Row cop is concerned primarily with peacekeeping and largely acts situationally, in response to the demands of the moment, the narc must structure his activity in order to build a case—drum up his own business, so to speak. The Skid Row cop has to rely on his observations and knowledge of his beat for decision-making guidance. The narc, on the other hand, has to rely on informers and undercover investigations to accomplish his goal. Moreover, whereas success to the Skid Row cop is measured largely in terms of how quiet he keeps his beat, for the narc the ultimate goal is the "big pinch" (catching a big-time pusher).

In short, arrest practices vary depending on the kind of activity the police deal with and the factors associated with that activity. Police officers who are routinely engaged in traffic control, for example, can be expected to behave somewhat differently from officers assigned to other kinds of activities. Hence, street patrol,

---

* For details regarding the behavior of police officers assigned to these different patrols see Bittner (1967) and Skolnick (1966:139-63).

investigative work, undercover work, riot control, etc. all occasion different styles of response.

Secondly, it appears that the "effectiveness" (i.e., arrest practices) of the police varies according to the structural organization of the department. While the over-all clearance rate for serious offenses is about 30 per cent, the rate differs considerably by type of crime. For example, violent crimes result in an arrest in approximately 45 per cent of the cases, as opposed to only 18 per cent of property crimes. As Table 1 demonstrates, arrest rates for the seven index crimes reported by the F.B.I. show a good deal of variation.

TABLE 1

Estimated Number of Arrests and
Percentage of Reported Crimes Cleared by an Arrest, U.S.A., 1971

Offense	Number of Arrests	Percentage of Reported Crimes
Murder	17,090	84%
Forcible Rape	20,120	55
Motor Vehicle Theft	157,100	16
Robbery	113,360	27
Aggravated Assault	172,120	66
Burglary	395,500	19
Larceny ($50+)	828,200	19

SOURCE: Adapted from the Federal Bureau of Investigation, 1971, p. 115, Table 23; p. 32, Chart 17.

Depending, of course, on the organizational structure of any police department, arrest and clearance rates can be expected to vary considerably. For instance, in a study comparing departments in two different towns with essentially the same population and social characteristics, Wilson (1968a) found that their rates of arrest varied a good deal. The basic differences between the two departments explain the difference in arrest rates. The East Coast city, which exhibited relatively low clearance rates, was a nonprofessional department. The officers in this department were poorly trained in police work, were not oriented to law enforcement, and tended to treat cases informally. In the West Coast city, however, the police were highly organized and trained and had a clear professional orientation. As a result, they were more likely to search actively for and detect lawbreakers and to arrest suspects rather than opt for an alternative disposition, such as giving the suspect a warning and sending him home. Hence, the arrest rates were comparatively high.

In another study, Wilson (1968) delineated three styles of police work: the *watchman* style, the *legalistic* style, and the *service* style. Although elements of all three can be found in any police department, different departments tend to emphasize one style more than the others and hence to practice different law-enforcement policies.

The watchman style emphasizes order maintenance as opposed to law enforcement, so that many minor infractions, especially if committed by juveniles or blacks, are either ignored or dealt with informally. Wilson comments (1968:140) that police operating in this type of department tend to

> . . . ignore many common minor violations, especially traffic and juvenile offenses, to tolerate, though gradually less so, a certain amount of vice and gambling, to use the law more as a means of maintaining order than of regulating conduct, and to judge the requirements of order differently depending on the character of the group in which the infraction occurs.

Underenforcement, corruption, and low arrest rates characterize watchman-style departments.

The legalistic style goes to the opposite extreme. Departments characterized by this style tend to treat all situations, even commonplace problems of maintaining order, as if they were matters of serious law infraction. Legalistic departments issue a high rate of traffic tickets, arrest a high proportion of juvenile offenders and misdemeanants, and crack down on illicit enterprises. Typically, the police act as if there were a single standard of conduct rather than different standards for different groups. Hence, some groups, especially juveniles, blacks, migrants, and others who tend not to live up to the police officers' conduct code, are more likely to feel the full wrath of law enforcement than are others considered more "respectable" in terms of the police definition of the term. Technical efficiency and high arrest rates characterize the legalistic style. The problem, however, is that this style breeds inequality in law enforcement, with harassment, brutality, and consequently frequent complaints from those groups most often subjected to police scrutiny.

Midway between the watchman and legalistic styles is the service style. In departments emphasizing a service orientation, the police seriously respond to all requests for either law enforcement or order maintenance. However, they are not geared to treating all cases in a formal manner. Apparently "the police see their chief responsibility as protecting a common definition of public order against the minor and occasional threats posed by unruly teenagers and 'outsiders'" (Wilson, 1968a:200). This style differs from the watchman style in that the police respond to all groups and apply informal sanctions in the case of minor offenses. It differs from the legalistic style in that fewer arrests are made for minor infractions and the police are more responsive to public sentiment and desires. In this sense, the service style is less arbitrary than the watchman style and more attuned to the practical considerations of public service than the legalistic style. As a result, citizen complaints against police in service departments tend to be low.

These two factors of police organization—unit assignment and departmental style—serve to condition police arrest practices. Coupled with the occupational function of police work common to all departments, these features provide a background for on-the-job decision-making. They do not, however, determine the actual decisions made in specific law-enforcement or order-maintenance situations.

Although variations in emphasis in terms of the factors just discussed can be found, how a given officer will treat a particular case depends not so much on departmental policy as on the officer's assessment of the situation. To explain a police officer's response to any particular situation, it is necessary to describe the elements that go into his world view or "occupational mentality." The police function and organization are significant to the extent that these factors help to condition or produce this world view.

POLICE DISCRETION

The characteristic feature of law enforcement—indeed, of the entire judicial process—is that legal officials have wide *discretion* (i.e., the freedom to make decisions on an individual basis) as to how and when they are to fulfill the occupational requirements of their office. Although it is commonly assumed and officially mandated that the police enforce all laws no matter what, in actual practice this would be impossible. Technically, the police simply lack the resources necessary for full law enforcement. Furthermore, most people probably would not favor a full law-enforcement policy. Socially, citizens would probably rebel against the kind of scrutiny required by full law enforcement, nor would they be willing to finance such a policy. Hence, the police are obliged to decide which laws are to be enforced and how much effort is to be given to enforcing some laws as opposed to others.

Law enforcement, therefore, is a matter of decision-making. Since the police occupy a position as first-line decision makers, they are significantly placed as far as the criminalization process is concerned. Whether they act on their own accord or in response to a citizen's complaint, the police are in a position to initiate the formal machinery that could result in someone's being defined as a criminal. While most police mobilizations are initiated by citizens who call the police to complain about some crime (Black and Reiss, 1970:66), it is the police who push the button. They may either arrest a suspect, release him, or invoke some other (informal) procedure. By choosing one or the other of these options, the police exercise a major influence in deciding what the law is and who the criminals are (Neiderhoffer, 1969:64). To account for police behavior, then, it is necessary that we describe the variable use of discretion made by the police.

The use of discretion can take a number of forms: investigative, confrontative, dispositional, and with regard to the use of force. That is, the police have the option (though limited) of investigating some acts and not others. The police, for example, may choose to ignore or actively pursue a citizen's complaint. Some people are treated with respect and politeness while others are abused. In some cases the police arrest a suspect while in others—even though the act and circumstances may be similar—the person is released. And some people are "roughed up" by the police while others are handled relatively gently. All along the line decisions are made by the police. Since these decisions have important consequences, the question of how they arrive at them is by no means unimportant.

The problem with discretionary law enforcement is that there is a thin line between discretion and discrimination. If the probability that a person will be socially recognized as a criminal is dependent on the discretionary power of the police to respond or ignore a citizen's complaint, arrest or release a suspect, and the like, then the probability that any one individual will be labeled a criminal increases or decreases depending on that person's correspondence to police conceptions of the criminal. Some people are more likely than others to have their behavior treated as crime by the police and, as a result, are more likely to receive a criminal identity. For example, Goldman (1963:35–47) discovered that 65 per cent of the black offenders apprehended by the police were referred to the Juvenile Court, but only 34 per cent of the white youths arrested received this treatment. In another study, Black and Reiss (1970:68) found that 21 per cent of the black youngsters encountered by the police, but only 8 per cent of the white youths, were arrested. Similarly, Skolnick (1966:71–90) observed that the police make discretionary (discriminatory?) decisions in the enforcement of traffic warrants. According to Skolnick, a much larger number of black offenders are arrested for failure to pay traffic fines than are whites, who are generally allowed to remain free and make payment at a later time.

Although the evidence is less than systematic, there is reason to believe that young adults, poor citizens, minority members, migrants, people who look disreputable, and the like are more severely treated by the police in that their activity is more likely to be scrutinized by the police and they are more likely to experience one or another form of police brutality and to be arrested than are more "respectable" citizens. It could, of course, be the case that individuals with these characteristics are in fact more criminalistic than is everyone else. Or they may more often be engaged in the kinds of serious illegality that are likely to draw police attention. On the other hand, differential arrest, surveillance, and treatment behavior on the part of the police could be the result of police prejudice. Before we can make a decision as to which, if either, of these conclusions is correct, it would be best to analyze police behavior in some detail.

THE POLICEMAN'S WORKING PERSONALITY

Each encounter a police officer has with a citizen is defined (assessed) by the officer from a perspective peculiar to law-enforcement officials. Moreover, how he handles a particular situation depends on the relation of the features of the situation to this perspective and the "tools" at his disposal to deal with an encounter. The principal tool available to the police is their authority as officers of the law. Basically, this means that police behavior revolves around the utilization of power. The sources of police power are both formal and informal. Formal power is derived from the law itself, the monopoly the police hold over the legitimate use of force to induce compliance, and their ability to make formal arrests. Informally, the police have power due to the illegal use of force, the general public respect for (fear of?) the police and the law, and the secrecy surrounding the police and their work.

Given these resources, the decision-making problem faced by the police centers on the absence of explicit guides or rules to which they may refer in employing their power. Also, in both law-enforcement and order-maintenance situations, the decision as to how to treat the encounter must usually be made on the spot. As a result, the police must rely on experience and intuition in arriving at an assessment of the encounter and how it is to be handled. For example, in disputes within the family, the rookie cop soon learns that an arrest is a waste of time, because the spouse is not likely to file a complaint. However, sometimes an arrest is the only expedient available to the police in dealing with the problem. The decision the police officer is likely to make in such cases depends largely on his own judgment. This judgment, in turn, not only is related to the concrete features of the case at hand but stems from, and is related to, the occupational ideology, or "focal concerns," of police work (Hartjen, 1972a).

Jerome Skolnick (1966:42–70) has described these occupational concerns in some detail. Most observers seem to agree that the behavior of police is largely a function of their concern over *danger, authority, hostility, efficiency,* and *suspicion.* Taken together, these concerns comprise the "working personality" of the police officer. That is, to the police the world is a dangerous and

hostile place. The people he is charged with protecting and controlling are defined by him as his enemies, ready and willing to
turn on him at any moment, so that each situation must be dealt
with cautiously. But at the same time, the police like to think of
themselves and show themselves as being efficient, competent
craftsmen. Moreover, the police officer conceives of himself as a
representative of the law. Indeed, in a practical sense, he *is* the
law. For the police, the procedural laws are but a set of working
conditions—stumbling blocks that impede effective (i.e., efficient)
police work—not something to be upheld for their own sake
(Skolnick, 1966:196; Bittner, 1967:713).

This occupational ideology colors the police officer's definition
of situations and thus ultimately affects who is officially defined
as a criminal. Although police activities are formally regulated by
procedural law, in practice police behavior conforms more closely
to this occupational code than to anything else. Hence, not only
are due-process rules regularly violated by the police in work-
aday encounters, but insofar as actual police behavior stems
from the occupational concerns of the police rather than from
some overt concern for the law, it can justly be said that the
police do not, in fact, enforce the law. *Law enforcement is but
a euphemism for a set of activities intended to satisfy the morality,
sense of propriety, and occupational ideology of the law enforcers
themselves.* For the police, the law is but one of the tools in their
work kit. It is something to be used when necessary to serve the
occupational concerns of police work. In this sense, law for the
police is a behavioral resource that serves to stimulate and
justify police action.

The main problem faced by the police in workaday encounters
is not how to enforce the law but when to use the law. That is,
when can the law be employed effectively and legitimately to
fulfill whatever concern emerges as problematic for the police?
Behaviorally, the law has been invoked when an arrest is made.
But what influences the use of arrest in concrete situations? To
discover the answer, we shall turn to the police-citizen encounter.

POLICE-CITIZEN ENCOUNTERS

In very few cases of law enforcement is there any clear evidence
either that a crime has been committed or that a particular per-

son is the perpetrator. As Quinney (1970a:124) suggests, in many cases "that which is defined as criminal is not so much behavior in obvious violation of a specific criminal law as it is a definition of circumstances that occur in the encounter between interacting parties in a concrete situation." In many cases in which an encounter culminates in an arrest, this decision results from a reasonable assessment on the part of the police that a crime has actually been committed and that the person arrested perpetrated the act. However, as LaFave (1965) demonstrates, there are a number of extralegal objectives for which the police use their arrest power. For example, a police officer may arrest a person simply in order to maintain respect for the police system. Suspects who are belligerent, do not show proper remorse or respect, or in other ways flout police authority are likely to be arrested to "teach them a lesson." In some cases a person may be arrested in order to maintain an image of full law enforcement. Typically this occurs when an offense that is usually treated informally or ignored comes to public attention, as in the case of backroom gambling clubs, prostitution, and the like. Sometimes an arrest is made simply to detain or punish a person who is suspected of other criminal activity. Sometimes the police will arrest a person on a minor charge in order to "get the goods on him" for a more serious offense. In yet other instances, an arrest will be made in order to ensure a person's safety. Drunks, for example, are routinely arrested as a preventive measure to protect them from harm.

LaFave's analysis implies that matters other than the behavior of a suspect frequently form the grounds for criminal arrest. Although this is true, the available evidence does suggest that the principal criterion for making an arrest decision is the seriousness of the act committed (e.g., Piliavin and Briar, 1964). Unless other factors mitigate the situation, the police will usually make an arrest in cases of serious law violations (provided, of course, that they can locate a suspect). On the other hand, minor offenses will usually be treated informally. As a general model, the seriousness of the behavior applies to most cases. However, in some cases, even when a serious violation has occurred, the suspect is released. On the other hand, sometimes a person is arrested for committing a minor crime even though the usual practice is to release such individuals. Under what conditions will one or the other of these choices be made?

A number of studies suggest that whether or not serious acts culminate in an arrest while minor acts are treated formally depends on two kinds of factors. One is the police officer's assessment of the suspect's basic "criminal character" (i.e., whether the policeman defines the suspect as a good guy gone wrong or as a "real" criminal). Second is the extent to which the suspect or his action conflicts with the police officer's occupational concerns. In part this factor relates to the first in the sense that a person who flouts police authority, exhibits hostility, or in other ways departs from the police officer's definition of proper deferential behavior is likely to be seen as more criminalistic than someone else—independent of the behavior involved.

The question is, on what do the police base their decisions in these matters? It appears that the police officer's assessment has to do with the suspect's personal characteristics (e.g., his dress, demeanor, age, race, group affiliations, and attitudes) and the offense or encounter circumstances, which involve the characteristics and desires of the complainant and the social setting of the encounter.

For example, in a now classic study, Piliavin and Briar (1964) demonstrated that, except for obviously serious cases, the dress and the demeanor of the youths encountered by the police were two of the more important cues employed by the officers to make an arrest decision. Juveniles who were uncooperative and hostile to the police were more likely to be arrested than cooperative youngsters, who were usually admonished and released. As Piliavin and Briar state:

> Older juveniles, members of known delinquent gangs, Negroes, youths with well-oiled hair, black jackets, and soiled denims or jeans (the presumed uniform of the "tough" boys), and the boys who in their interactions with officers did not manifest what were considered to be appropriate signs of respect tended to receive the more severe dispositions [p. 210].

Although only a few of the encounters the police had with juveniles resulted in an arrest, according to the studies of Black and Reiss (1970), a higher proportion of black youngsters than of whites received this disposition. The probability that a youngster would be arrested depended on the seriousness of the offense, the evidence available, and the demeanor of the juvenile. However, black youngsters were more likely to be arrested than white youths independent of these factors.

Black and Reiss argue that the differences in arrest rates between the two groups can be explained in terms of the desires of the complainant. While the decision to arrest or release a suspect ultimately is a matter for the police officer's discretion, generally police mobilizations are initiated by some citizen complainant, not by the police themselves. Hence, the outcome of a police-citizen encounter is influenced to some extent, at least, by the person initiating the interaction. In cases where no complainant was present, the arrest rates for blacks and whites were practically the same. However, when a complainant was present, black youths were almost two and a half times more likely to be arrested. Generally it was found that the complainant was of the same race as the juvenile, and the police tended to adhere to the wishes of the complainant. If the complainant wanted the police to be lenient, the police were lenient. If he wanted the police to make an arrest, he got an arrest. Black and Reiss concluded that the differential arrest rates for black and white youth were in part a consequence of the encounter situation. More black complainants requested that the police arrest an offender of the same race.

In an investigation of police referral decisions for juveniles, Ferdinard and Luchterhand (1970) found that of those offenders arrested, 63 per cent of the white youngsters and 76 per cent of the black juveniles were referred to the juvenile court. This difference could not be explained by the seriousness of the youths' behavior, their attitudes, or their demeanor. Apparently, since the police were white, they tended to be less familiar with the black youngsters and used more superficial evidence (such as the juveniles' style of dressing) to decide their fates. Because they were more familiar with white juveniles, they employed more refined criteria to decide their fates.

A study dealing with adult arrest rates (Green, 1970) suggests a similar conclusion. According to Green, white males over the age of 25 who held low-status jobs and were migrants to the area contributed the lion's share to the group of people arrested. However, when absolute numbers are converted to arrest rates for blacks and whites, it was found that a disproportionate number of blacks are arrested, independent of any other factor. This does not mean that racial factors are necessarily associated with either behavioral patterns or police attitudes; the arrest differences do not necessarily reflect differences in the relative criminality of the two groups or police prejudice toward blacks. Rather, the differences in arrest rates may be a function of the differences between the two populations in occupational and nativity characteristics. Lower-class and migrant whites and blacks are equally subject to arrest. Hence, Green concluded that the higher arrest rates for blacks reflected the fact that a higher proportion of the black community was employed in low-status jobs or had recently migrated to the area.

Of course, this does not mean that discrimination is not involved here. To the extent that factors related to arrest are in turn related to racial discrimination, the differences in arrest rates are ultimately an expression of that discrimination. That is, if unemployed persons are more likely to be arrested than employed persons, and if a black man cannot get a job because of racial discrimination, then the higher probability of his being arrested is a function of the discriminatory conditions that place him in a high arrest probability category.

CONCLUSION

It is clear that different segments of the population have different probabilities of having their behavior labeled criminal by the police. Hence, they have different probabilities of being formally and socially identified as criminal persons. Although a suspect's behavior is of primary importance in determining his chances of being arrested, in most cases the decision to arrest a person is based on factors that have little to do with the degree of a person's behavioral criminality. Moreover, the evidence suggests that the factors affecting arrest decision-making are grounded in and reflect something other than law-enforcement goals. If, therefore, it is not so much what a person does as what kind of person he is (or is seen by the police to be) that affects official labeling, then the notion of equitable and impartial justice is nothing but a myth. The label *criminal* is no more than a symbolic evaluation of a person's character, not of his behavior. Crime, therefore, is but one way societal members have of supporting their own image of moral virtue, an image that is created by and demonstrated in the act of arrest. For the person arrested, arrest is but the beginning of a process—a process geared to demonstrating that what the act of arrest presupposes is the case in fact.

5

The Process of Criminal Justice

THE FUNCTIONAL PURPOSE of our present-day judicial machinery is to act as a kind of board of review over police arrest behavior. As we have seen, a person may be introduced to the system of criminal justice for a number of reasons. The role of the police in the criminalization process is all but completed once an arrest has been made, except when additional investigative work is required or when they have to appear as witnesses to support their allegations. After an arrest has been made, the suspect comes under the jurisdiction of the court, and it is for the court to rule on the correctness of the police decision to arrest. A continuation of the case by the act of prosecution is essentially an affirmation of police suspicions.

Most people probably have limited, if any, direct contact with the criminal courts. The image of the judicial process held by most Americans is therefore gained largely from the mass media. Dramatic confessions *à la* Perry Mason do occur in real-life criminal cases, but only rarely. Undoubtedly some lawyers defend some cases without considering their fee—occasionally. Undoubtedly the idealized version of the search for truth and justice portrayed by the mass media is reflected in real criminal cases—infrequently. But the picture suggested by television dramas is, at best, a limited description of what actually transpires in the bulk of criminal cases. What in fact happens to a suspect after arrest? Why, and under what conditions, are some suspects prosecuted and others released? How are sentences decided? What factors influence the activity of defense lawyers, judges, juries, and prosecutors? These and similar questions are today the topics of research by a number of social scientists and legal scholars.

AMERICAN COURT STRUCTURE AND PROCEDURES

Any statement made about the American system of criminal justice in general is, by definition, an overgeneralization, because there is no single judicial system existing in America today. Indeed, over time, our judicial system has developed in a rather piecemeal fashion. Nor did the same system evolve throughout the country. As the authors of the President's Commission on Law Enforcement and Administration of Justice (1967:7) point out: "Every village, town, county, city, and state has its own criminal-justice system, and there is a federal one as well. All of them operate somewhat alike. No two of them operate precisely alike." In fact, the court system can more rightly be called a nonsystem, for a sizable number and variety of courts hear cases dealing with criminal and other matters, some on a part-time and others on a full-time basis.

In the simplest sense, the court system consists of two main bodies: state and federal courts. Federal courts have three levels, from district courts to courts of appeals to the U. S. Supreme Court. The district courts have jurisdiction over cases arising from violations of federal law as well as those that occur in Washington, D.C., or on federal property; the higher courts not only hear appeals but can intervene in the affairs of state courts when constitutional issues are involved. Most criminal cases, however, are dealt with on a local level by state courts. There are two types of state courts: trial courts and appellate courts. Trial courts are concerned primarily with deciding the innocence or guilt of criminal defendants and matters of sentencing. In most states there are lower (or inferior) and higher trial courts. State appellate courts, like the federal high courts, are courts of review, acting in a policy-making capacity and deciding issues of due process. Usually each state has several appellate courts besides a state supreme court.

Judicial processing in most states follows a rather standard formal procedure. As the San Francisco Committee on Crime reports (in Kaplan, 1973:65–69), typically a person begins the process by the act of arrest. If the charge is felony (a crime for which a person can be sentenced to one year or more in prison), a person can be arrested in either of two ways: The police may swear a written complaint before a judge, who then issues a warrant for arrest; or the police can make an arrest without a warrant if they have "reasonable cause" to believe the person committed a felony. In the case of a misdemeanor, however, the police are usually required to have observed the act or a citizen must file a complaint. As the news media have recently publicized with regard to political corruption, an arrest may also follow from a preliminary investigation initiated by a district attorney or a grand jury, culminating in formal accusations and a warrant for the accused person's arrest. This procedure may also be initiated by a citizen's complaint to the district attorney.

Once the arrest has been made, the raw materials for the court to process have been supplied. Some of the individuals arrested for criminal offenses are dispensed with early in the process. A few others, however, receive the royal treatment, being required (or allowed) to face every stage of the formal process outlined below.

The second step in the formal processing of criminal defendants is the *booking*, at which time the initial charges against the person are recorded, his fingerprints are taken, and the like. It is at this point in the procedure that the person acquires an official "rap sheet," or record, an occurrence that can have severe consequences for his future life no matter what the ultimate outcome of the case may be. After the booking, the case is turned over to the district attorney, who files a written *complaint*, unless, of course, he decides to drop the case entirely. At this stage the defendant may consult his attorney and be released on bail. But whether or not a person is released on bail or held in jail, he must be taken before a magistrate without delay for a *preliminary hearing*. Usually this takes place in one of the inferior courts. Following the preliminary hearing, either the case is dismissed or *formal charges* are brought against the individual. This usually occurs in one of two ways. The district attorney may present the case to a grand jury, which issues an *indictment,* or he may simply issue an *information* specifying the charges against the individual. Once formal charges have been brought, the case is taken from the inferior court and transferred to the superior court for prosecution.

On his first encounter with the superior court, the defendant faces a process called *arraignment,* in which the charges against him are read, an attorney is assigned if the defendant has been without one so far, and a plea can be entered concerning the charges. Usually the plea is postponed until the defendant's next appearance before the court. If he pleads guilty to all the charges, *sentencing* is pronounced. Again, this is usually postponed. If, however, the defendant pleads not guilty, his lawyer may, at this point, make several pretrial *motions** before the court. A date is set to hear the motions, and on this occasion, a decision on the motions is rendered by the judge.

The case now goes to *trial.* In most jurisdictions the defendant may choose to be tried by jury rather than a judge or a panel of judges. The first step in the jury-trial proceedings is *selection of the jury.* Once this is accomplished, the actual trial can begin. Following the trial the jury presents its findings. If a finding of "guilty" is returned, a date is set for *sentencing.* The last appearance the convicted defendant makes before the court involves sentencing, which can involve suspension of a prison term, probation, a fine (rare in jury cases), or commitment to prison. Following conviction and sentencing, a defendant can appeal his case to a higher court.

This is the basic outline for processing criminal cases in American state and federal courts. In fact, however, very few defendants ever go through the entire process, many steps are bypassed, and a number of alternative dispositions can take place at various points in the process. (E.g., see Figure 2, pp. 12–13.) To what extent judicial processing as it actually takes place conforms to

---

* For example, the defense can request that all (or some) of the charges be dropped or modified, that evidence be suppressed, or that the defense be granted access to evidence held by the prosecution.

one's conception of criminal justice depends, of course, on one's image or model of criminal justice.

THE NOTION OF JUSTICE

There are various conceptions of justice contained in the philosophical literature and writings on jurisprudence. For some people justice simply means receiving one's "just deserts." For others, it is something quite different. What is clear, however, is that the administration of criminal law must rest on *some* implicit notion of what justice involves. An analysis of judicial procedure as it routinely takes place in criminal cases may reveal what this unstated conception is and the role it plays in the creation of socially recognized criminal persons.

It is also clear that, when competing conceptions of the nature of justice exist, the machinery of justice will be subjected to criticism by one group or another. This appears to be the case in present-day American society. The late Herbert L. Packer (1968: 154–73), for example, suggested that the administration of criminal justice is complicated by the competition between two opposing value systems which underlie alternative approaches to the judicial process. These values, which Packer called the *crime-control* model and the *due-process* model, represent, in effect, polar extremes regarding the nature of justice. Neither model exists in pure form. Elements of both characterize our present judicial system in America, although specific cases tend to be dealt with more in terms of one of these models than the other. Also, under recent administrations there appears to be some tendency to promote the crime-control model at the expense of due-process considerations. Since adherence to one or the other of these value systems can have grave implications for the disposition of "justice" in American society, it is worthwhile to detail Packer's analysis in some depth.

The Crime-Control Model According to Packer, underlying the notion of crime control is the proposition that repression of criminal conduct is by far the most important function of criminal justice. Advocates of this model claim that the criminal-justice process exists to ensure social freedom. To secure the greatest amount of this freedom, authorities must produce a high rate of arrests and convictions. Speed and finality in handling cases are at a premium, requiring the use of informal procedures and the uniform disposition of similar cases. Where due-process rules block the disposition of a case, the criminal court, like the police, dispenses with the rules. In short, the crime-control model requires that cases be categorized and handled in a routine way so far as is possible.

The image that comes to mind regarding this model is an assembly-line conveyor-belt system in which individuals are "sorted" by a series of routinized operations geared to processing each case to its ultimate conclusion, whether this leads to justice or injustice, to acquittal or conviction, and then proceeding to the next case.

The assumption underlying the successful operation of this model in practice is the presumption of guilt. The presumption of guilt is not, Packer suggests, opposite to the presumption of innocence. That is, it is not necessary under the presumption of innocence to actually assume that a suspect is, in fact, innocent until proved guilty. Rather, the presumption of innocence acts as a guide for official action, requiring that until a person is duly found guilty he must be treated "as if" his guilt were an open question.

As Packer makes clear, the presumption of guilt which is necessary for the successful operation of the crime-control model is purely and simply a prediction of outcome. Having already screened out all cases that would probably not result in a successful conviction, the crime-control model operates on the assumption that all the remaining cases *are* guilty. The entire process is designed to carry this assumption through to completion as fast as possible. The principal device employed by the court to secure this result is the plea of guilty.

The Due-Process Model   The due-process model of justice can almost be described as the exact opposite of the ideology of crime control. Whereas a system governed by the desire to repress crime would resemble a people-processing assembly line, the due-process approach would have the features of an obstacle course for judicial authorities. The essential distinction between the two is that the crime-control model tends to rely on the police and the public prosecutor to make dispositional decisions, whereas the due-process model rejects the absolute authority of these officials and requires that formal, adjudicative, advisory-type fact-finding procedures be followed. The crime-control model seeks to convict the probably guilty and hence strives for efficiency. On the other hand, the due-process model desires to protect the probably innocent and hence strives for reliability. In this sense, the crime-control model emphasizes "production" and the due-process model "quality control."

Another difference centers on the ideological distinction between the two approaches. The crime-control model sees the essential task of the judicial machinery as that of protecting the people from one another and the state from the people. The advocates of due process, however, are geared to protecting the people from the coercive power of the state. These different philosophies lead to the employment of different tactics in administering criminal justice. Advocates of crime control, for example, complain that the police are rendered ineffective to fight crime by the procedural protections of due process. Hence, they lobby for wiretapping, the use of informers, the use of forced confessions, and the like. Adherents of the philosophy of due process contend just the opposite. They seek to place controls on the state to prevent it from operating at peak efficiency. Maximal efficiency, they argue, is maximal tyranny.

Finally, whereas the crime-control model is rooted in the presumption of guilt, the central idea underlying the due-process model is the doctrine of "legal guilt." A person caught redhanded while mugging an eighty-year-old woman may indeed be "factually guilty" of theft. But this does not necessarily mean that he is "legally guilty." A person's legal guilt is only partially dependent on his factual guilt. According to the idea of due process, legal guilt is something to be determined by the court, and this can be done only if the factual determination of guilt is made in a procedurally regular fashion by authorities competent to make that decision acting within the powers allocated to them by the state. Moreover, even if a person is factually guilty, he cannot be held legally guilty if any of the rules of procedure designed to protect him in the process of making that determination are violated.

JUDICIAL PROCESSING

We have already seen that most offenses known to the police do not culminate in an arrest. Of those offenders actually arrested on criminal charges, probably fewer than half are formally charged. Most cases are, it would seem, disposed of in some informal manner. There are a number of reasons why cases are dropped, including mistaken arrest, insufficient evidence to warrant prosecution, withdrawal of complaint, disappearance of witnesses, refusal of witnesses to testify, and the like. However, the majority of those charged with a crime do wind up being convicted. This also may be the result of a number of factors, such as bargaining practices, the elimination of weak cases early in the proceedings, and pressures placed on defendants to cop a plea. As Table 2 indicates, fewer than 20 per cent of the more than two million persons charged with crimes in 1971 were acquitted of these charges. This statistic, of course, varies by type of crime; property offenders are less likely to be acquitted than are personal offenders. In the case of drunkenness, for which over 600,000 arrests were made in 1971, over 90 per cent were convicted as charged. Persons accused of negligent manslaughter, however, were convicted at a much lower rate; only 34 per cent of the 790 persons charged with this offense were found guilty (the Federal Bureau of Investigation, 1971:110).

TABLE 2

Disposition of Formally Charged Persons, 1971

| | No. of Charges | % Guilty | | % Acquitted or Dismissed | % Juvenile Court |
		As Charged	Lesser Crime		
Total	2,251,647	61	4	17	18
Violent Crimes	65,603	30	13	30	28
Property Crimes	341,046	39	6	15	41

SOURCE: The Federal Bureau of Investigation (1971:110, Table 15).

The President's Commission on Law Enforcement and Administration of Justice (1967:121–28) found results similar to those reported by the FBI. Of the 5,258 felony cases processed in Detroit in 1967, fewer than one fifth (13 per cent, N=708) were handled by a trial, and only 34 per cent (N=243) of these were tried by a jury. Moreover, in 74 per cent (N=3,828) of all the cases processed, a conviction was obtained. Of those tried who were not convicted, fewer than 9 per cent (N=115) were acquitted by a trial; the rest were either dismissed by the court or not prosecuted. It is significant that in over 85 per cent (N=3,235) of the cases convicted, conviction was due to a plea of guilty.

It is obvious from these figures that the model of criminal justice that most closely fits actual judicial processing is the crime-control model. In fact, the administration of justice in the United States today largely resembles an assembly-line operation involving informal, routine, summary kinds of treatment of criminal defendants. Anyone who has been issued a traffic summons or spent an evening observing night court has experienced but a small portion of a much more pervasive system that operates in similar ways even in more serious cases. The cornerstone of this whole procedure is the guilty plea.

PROSECUTION AND THE PROSECUTOR

The significance of the plea of guilty to criminal charges can best be understood by considering the officials who routinely extract this plea from persons accused of criminal conduct. The key figure in this is the public prosecutor, the district attorney. As the figures reported above indicate, probably the most important decision in judicial processing (at least as far as the defendant is concerned) is the decision to prosecute a person on criminal charges. This decision rests largely with the prosecutor.

Lawyers and criminologists have long realized that the prosecutor is the principal personage in the judicial apparatus. Compared to the prosecutor, the judge under ordinary circumstances has but a small and largely ritualistic role to play in criminal cases. In fact, the prosecutor is probably one of the most powerful officials in the entire governmental structure. Surprisingly little is known, however, about prosecutors and the bases for their behavior.

It appears that much of the prosecutor's work is influenced by political and bureaucratic considerations. Because most prosecutors are elected to their office, at least at the local level, and because most use their office as a stepping stone to higher political positions, they are usually sensitive to public attitudes. Like the police, the prosecutor has a wide range of discretion in deciding how he will exercise his powers. Not only does he have the option to decide whether or not to prosecute, but he can determine which charges will be brought against an individual and which, if any, will be changed as the proceedings progress. His discretion regarding whether or not to bring formal charges is probably the most important of his powers. Of major sociological interest is the basis on which this power is exercised.

In a study of assistant district attorneys, John Kaplan (1968: 230–39) reports that the major problem confronting these prosecutors is how to make the most effective use of limited time, energy, and resources while staying out of trouble with superiors. Required to process a large number of cases with mostly inadequate resources, the assistant D.A.s have developed a tacit set of standards for making these decisions. According to Kaplan, the most basic and important of these standards is the prosecutor's assessment of the accused individual's guilt or innocence of the charge. Regardless of the strength of the case, if the prosecutors believed the accused was not guilty, they generally felt it morally wrong to press for prosecution. (This inhibition, of course, could be relaxed in special cases.)

If the D.A.s felt the accused was guilty, an important consideration that influenced their decision to prosecute was the possibility of obtaining a conviction. Prosecution was rarely undertaken unless the prosecutor believed the chances of success (a conviction) were better than even. There are a number of reasons that prosecutors wanted to prosecute only potentially successful cases. Primary among these is the D.A.'s concern about wasting time and money. But "personal" reasons—preserving the D.A.'s record and reputation among his colleagues—are also involved.

In another study George F. Cole (1970) investigated the decision to prosecute among deputy prosecutors of Seattle, Washington. According to Cole, this decision is, in part at least, influenced by such external factors and forces as police pressures, court congestion, community attitudes, and organizational considerations.

The rather limited picture we can discern from these and similar investigations suggests that a number of extralegal factors enter into the decision to prosecute, often emanating from the prosecutor's occupational and political concerns rather than reflecting features of the actual case being handled. In short, whether or not the defendant is really guilty may have little to do with the decision to prosecute or to dismiss the case entirely.

It says something about our judicial system that a prosecutor's decision to invoke the criminal process depends on whether or not he thinks he would look silly before a jury or whether or not prosecution of that case will damage or enhance his chances in the next election. Erving Goffman (1959) once argued that people who become mental patients probably "suffer" more from "career contingencies" than they do from actual mental pathology. That is, the likelihood that a person will be committed to a mental institution depends more on a number of contingency factors (e.g., the availability of space) than on the person's actual mental state. From what is known about how people are selected for the social identity "criminal," Goffman's statement aptly applies to judicial processing as well. Embarking on a "career" as an officially recognized "criminal" is, to be sure, largely contingent on the discretion of the prosecutor. The problem is that this discretion differentially falls on certain segments of the population—namely, the poor and powerless. How these people are treated by our legal institutions reveals better than anything else the workings of our judicial system.

DEFENDING THE POOR IN CRIMINAL CASES

It has been estimated that over 300,000 persons annually are charged with serious crimes (felonies) and that over half of the people so charged cannot afford the services of a lawyer to defend them. Of the others, most can afford to pay only part of a lawyer's fees and other expenses of an adequate defense (Silverstein, 1965: 7). Defending oneself against serious criminal charges is a costly business and, except for a very few, places a severe financial burden on the defendant. Who, without sacrifice, can afford the several hundred dollars it usually costs for even a nominal defense in a criminal case—a financial burden for which defendants are rarely, if ever, compensated no matter how the case turns out? For the poor, and indeed for the average citizen, defending oneself against the accusations of the state is economically an impossible task. Yet, as the large majority of persons who face criminal charges are poor, it goes without saying that the weight of the criminal-justice system rests most heavily on the shoulders of the underprivileged classes of our society.*

It is a historical fact that the legal institution—while professing equality before the law—has always favored the rich over the poor. It is true that in many respects the law and legal procedures have been constituted so as to keep the poor person in his place. Miller (1966: 389), for example, suggests that in the United States white men have long been legally classified on the basis of economic distinctions. Slaves, of course, because they were excluded from owning property, were generally not covered by the laws protecting their masters. Yet even for the dominant white population, the economic classifications embodied in the law were so designed as to impair equality. Property contingencies determining one's right to vote or hold public office, the imprisonment of debtors, vagabonds, and others (simply because of their economic status), and the practice of forcing a poor person to face criminal prosecution without a lawyer are but a few of the features of our early legal system that institutionalized inequality.

It can, of course, be argued that many of these inequalities have been abolished or, at least, alleviated over the years by Supreme Court rulings which have sought to extend the Bill of Rights to cases not specifically covered by federal statute. For example, recent Court decisions have in large measure rectified the problem of representation, and other steps have been taken to secure the rights guaranteed by the Constitution to indigent defendants. In the case of *Gideon* v. *Wainwright,* the Court ruled that a lawyer must be provided for a person without funds who is charged with a felony if his case goes to trial. This provision was eventually extended to persons who plead guilty and thus waive their right to a jury trial—a situation that involves nearly 90 per cent of all criminal cases. In the case of *Escobedo* v. *Illinois,* the Court pursued this line of thought even further by ruling that counsel must be provided prior to police interrogation of a suspect. Finally, in *Miranda* v. *Arizona,* it was decided that a

* For an excellent description of how poor defendants of various kinds are handled in criminal cases, see Wald, 1967.

defendant not only must be granted his constitutional rights but must also be advised by the police at the time of arrest as to what these rights are.

These and similar decisions have done much to make a reality of the ideals expressed in the Constitution. The question still remains, however, whether lawyers supplied to poor defendants are doing the kind of job that retained counsel would (or should) do for wealthy clients. In attempting to answer this question, a review of the system of criminal defense and the role of the defense attorney, especially as it applies to defending poor persons, may be helpful.

There are a variety of systems for supplying indigent defendants with attorneys. The most common methods are the *assigned counsel* system (by which the court appoints a lawyer to a case with nominal compensation) and the *public defender* system. Public defenders are paid a salary by the state and usually work out of an office established for the exclusive purpose of representing poor citizens. Although it is not yet clear which of these systems is preferable, limited data suggest that the public-defender system is slightly better as far as the adequacy of the defense supplied is concerned (Benjamin and Pedeliski, 1969). However, how the defense offered by a public defender compares with that provided by a retained lawyer has yet to be determined. There is reason to suspect that even though defendants with privately retained lawyers may fare somewhat better, the differences are negligible, on the whole, given the kinds of lawyers who tend to specialize in criminal cases and the kind of practice this usually generates for them.

In one of the most exhaustive and revealing studies of legal-defense systems, Silverstein (1965) found that persons requiring supplied counsel were placed in a disadvantageous position at the very outset of judicial processing. For example, defendants in need of public defenders were assigned attorneys late in the proceedings, were uninformed of their judicial rights, and in general were treated in a discriminatory manner by the court which assigned the attorneys.

What is suggested by the research regarding criminal defense is that, even though it may seem that some defense is better than none at all, by whatever means it is supplied, the simple act of supplying a lawyer offers no assurance that the defense will be adequate. In many cases supplying a lawyer may result in a total lack of justice. In short, if the attorney's orientation and goal are something other than the best interests of his client, much less the pursuit of justice, it may be advantageous for the defendant to have no counsel at all.

THE GUILTY PLEA

The principal method of adjudicating criminal cases in the United States is by a plea of guilty. As we have noted, on the average, approximately 90 per cent of all cases are handled in this manner. It is recognized that the judicial system in America as it is presently organized would probably cease to operate at all were all cases brought to trial. The system is simply not designed to cope with such a contingency.

Most guilty pleas result from a process of negotiation; thus the ultimate disposition of a case is more a matter of bargaining over charges and sentences than anything else. For example, in one study Donald Newman (1956) found that most defendants who initially pleaded not guilty but later changed to a guilty plea did so as a result of an agreement struck between them and the prosecutor concerning the charges and/or sentence to be received. Those offenders who successfully bargained for a lesser charge or a lighter sentence were more frequently represented by an attorney. Defendants who were successful only in bargaining for concurrent sentences or for the dropping of some charges more often lacked an attorney to represent them.

Similar results were obtained in Silverstein's (1965) research. Silverstein's study is significant because it casts some light on the differences between having a supplied lawyer and a retained counsel. Although most defendants eventually pleaded guilty anyway, the supplied-counsel defendants pleaded guilty more often than did the clients of private attorneys. Also, retained-counsel defendants pleaded guilty to lesser offenses more frequently than did supplied-counsel defendants. With regard to the disposition of the case, it was found that clients represented by a court-appointed attorney were more often sentenced to a term in prison than were those represented by a private attorney.

The conclusion to be drawn from these and similar studies is

obvious. It is standard practice for all lawyers (supplied or retained) to negotiate a guilty plea in criminal cases (plea bargaining) and avoid a trial. Moreover, even though there are some
differences in the dispositions awarded to defendants accused of
similar crimes, the differences are not likely to be a function of
the kinds of lawyers the defendants have.

From the limited research available, it appears that at least
two major variables are important in plea bargaining. One has to
do with the legal practice of criminal law itself. The other stems
from the structure of indigent defense systems. As far as the legal
processing of poor defendants is concerned, the latter factor
appears more significant.

It is not unreasonable to assume that in order for an attorney
to gain full advantage for his client, his central interest (within
the ethical confines of his profession) must be the welfare and, if
possible, the acquittal of his client. In short, an adequate defense
requires, at minimum, a client-centered defense. It is not yet clear
to what extent defense attorneys of various kinds actively pursue
the best interests of their clients, but in a study of the public
defender's office, Sudnow (1965) found that the focus of orientation and involvement for the public defender is anything but the
client. Rather, it is centered on the courtroom and the affairs of
the court.

Legal philosophy, the model of due process, and the public
image of criminal justice all envision a combative system in
which the prosecutor and defense attorney "fight it out" in open
court in the interest of truth, justice, and humanity. The harsh
reality of the criminal-court system is somewhat different from
this image. Few cases are ever "fought out" in open court. Most
cases are "settled" outside of court, usually to the satisfaction of
all concerned. In those cases that do go to trial, the prosecutor
and defense attorney are rarely locked in mortal combat over the
fate of the defendant. As Sudnow indicates with regard to the
relationship between public defender and prosecuting attorney,
the "combatants" in the judicial system can better be described
as "conspirators" who work together to dispose expediently of the
chronically overburdened affairs of the court.

Apparently, the defense and prosecuting attorneys share a
common orientation to the court and a common conception of

the typical defendant. Both are concerned with obtaining a guilty plea whenever possible. At the same time, both are concerned that the defendant receive his "due," (in the sense of "just desserts") so neither is willing to be excessively lenient simply to induce the defendant to plead guilty and clear the court docket. Rather, they work together to negotiate a "reasonable" penalty, one that more or less complies with *their* conception of a just penalty for a particular kind of defendant.

Although research is lacking to substantiate the claim, it seems that the prevailing attitude among all participants in the court system is that persons brought before the court on criminal charges are "obviously" guilty of crimes. They may not have committed the particular crime with which they are charged. But they must, it is assumed, have done something wrong at some time; otherwise they wouldn't be there. And they are treated according to this preconception.*

It is probably also the case that both the public defender and the district attorney conspire together not so much because they seek to "do in" some defendant—although this does sometimes occur—but in order to ensure the smooth operation of the court system itself. Cases are practical problems (as opposed to legal matters), to be solved with due consideration for the burdens of the court. Thus, the defense attorney seldom exerts himself to secure an acquittal for his client. Sudnow states that "stubborn defendants" who insist on their innocence, who "will not listen to reason" and plead guilty, and who thus force a trial are given a "proper defense," but not a defense designed to win an acquittal. On the contrary, the defense lawyer goes through the motions of a defense. Court procedures are followed, and all the correct motions are made. But rarely is a hostile witness discredited. Rarely are the state's accusations refuted with vigor. Rarely does the defense cause trouble for the court or unnecessary delay for the system. When the defendant winds up receiving a harsher penalty than he would have received had he acquiesced and agreed to a guilty plea, it is, after all, what he deserved!

The energies of supplied counsel appear to be directed toward the workings of the court rather than the welfare of his client.

* Compare this description with the features of the philosophy underlying the crime-control model as outlined by Packer (1968).

This orientation is the key to understanding how supplied counsel carries out a defense. A disinterested attitude on the part of defense attorneys toward their clients coupled with the preassumption of guilt can only be aggravated by the practice of assigning defense counsel to a court rather than an individual client. As Sudnow notes, a defendant in a criminal case may be "represented" by a different attorney at every stage of judicial processing. Typically, the assigned lawyer has little contact or communication with his client. He relies on the defendant's file to supply him with all relevant information on which to base his defense. All he knows about his client is what the file tells him, and usually this tells him very little about his client. The statement of a defendant quoted by Casper (1972:101) vividly summarizes these points. When asked if he had a lawyer when he went to court, he remarked: "No, I had a public defender."

What about defendants represented by a private attorney? It has already been suggested that privately retained lawyers produce results not significantly different from those received when a person has a public defender. In many cases the lawyers who deal with criminal matters are among the least qualified and least prestigious members of the legal profession. Although this situation is apparently changing, criminal law is still looked down upon by many members of the legal profession as "dirty work." Moreover, it is an aspect of legal practice that is notorious for highly unethical and unprofessional, if not illegal, dealings. Many lawyers avoid this kind of practice except when necessary, as when a wealthy client is involved in some high-level white-collar crime like tax evasion, antitrust violation, or stock manipulation (see, e.g., Carlin, 1962). As a result, most defense attorneys who deal with the typical "garden variety" criminal case are drawn from a group of people known as solo lawyers (i.e., single practitioners rather than members of a firm). Solo lawyers themselves fall into two categories: those who specialize in criminal cases (regulars) and those who occasionally deal with clients facing criminal charges. Wood (1967) found that lawyers who specialize in criminal law tend to have come from relatively low socio-economic backgrounds, had inferior legal training, experienced difficulty getting started in legal practice, and are generally dissatisfied with the practice of criminal law.

Besides being undesirable from a professional perspective, the practice of criminal law is not particularly rewarding in an economic sense. Obviously most of the people requiring legal services in criminal cases are not wealthy. Most have few if any assets with which to pay an attorney, so that, as Blumberg (1967) points out, one of the principal problems faced by the criminal lawyer is the task of setting and collecting his fee, not to mention convincing his client that he earned it. This results, Blumberg argues, in the subordination of the lawyer's concern for justice to the simple business of making a living. Thus, a legal career based on criminal cases necessitates a volume business and the expeditious handling of cases. Long-drawn-out trials requiring specialized witnesses must be avoided. Fast settlement based on plea bargaining becomes almost an economic necessity.

Most lawyers specializing in criminal law are tied to the judicial machinery as a referral source. It is necessary, therefore, that such attorneys (except those associated with some organization like Legal Aid) maintain congenial relationships with elements of the structure to ensure future clients. These attorneys are not, as a result, likely to alienate prosecutors, judges, and other officials by disrupting court routine, regardless of their client's interests. This situation places criminal lawyers (particularly solo criminal lawyers) in a moral bind. While appeasing the court, they must, at the same time, persuade their clients that they are getting results and protecting the clients' interests. A subtle game is thus played in which lawyers employ subterfuge to maintain their clients' confidence while manipulating them to accept a workable compromise. Regardless of their own moral or judicial orientation toward the idea of justice, most criminal lawyers are enmeshed in a situation in which legal ethics must be compromised by the simple requirements of maintaining a practice. In short, whereas the public defender is often the lackey of the judicial system, many a solo criminal lawyer has become its stooge.

TRIAL BY JURY

Although the vast majority of criminal cases reach adjudication by means of a plea of guilty, sometimes cases do come to trial, and some of these cases are tried before a jury. The right to trial by jury is guaranteed to all felony defendants by the U.S. Constitution, and in some states it is available in minor cases as well. Usually defendants can choose to have their case heard by a judge, a panel of judges, or a jury. On the average, fewer than one out of seven felony prosecutions are actually tried by a jury. This figure, to be sure, varies considerably by type of crime and from jurisdiction to jurisdiction. Yet, the fact remains, jury trials are drastically underutilized in American criminal courts, even though some 80 per cent of all jury trials in the world occur in American criminal cases (Kalven and Zeisel, 1966:12–32).

This does not demean the importance of the jury or the influence it may have over criminal prosecutions. No matter what pressure is exerted on the defendant to plead guilty, the possibility always exists that he will refuse and insist on a jury trial. Thus, pretrial decisions must be conducted with an eye on what the jury might do. In this respect, the jury serves to control the informal bargaining process designed to bypass the trial as a mode of handling criminal cases.

The jury has long been the subject of debate, but it is only of late that it has been subjected to empirical research. Two major issues have been raised regarding the jury. One criticism centers on the competence of jurors to decide complex issues of law. The other concerns possible prejudice on the part of jurors. To date the limited data do not permit resolution of these controversies, although some light can be thrown on the jury's composition and functioning.

According to Kalven and Zeisel (1966:494–96), the activity of the jury is directed in large part to deciding issues of fact and weighing the evidence. Moreover, it appears that juries are no less competent to decide cases than are judges, since the judge and jury were in agreement as to the disposition of the cases 75 per cent of the time. Yet, in two thirds of the cases in which the judge and jury disagreed, the jury appeared to be responding to other than factual matters and was being influenced by values external to the legal aspects of the case. The authors argue that these values were employed only in the resolution of problems concerning evidence. In this regard, the study also suggests that no apparent directionality colors the jury's decisions. The jury, that is, is disposed neither for nor against the defendant.

But these findings do not preclude the influence of bias in jury deliberations. As any trial lawyer knows, the individual juror's background and personal characteristics do influence the way in which the jury will respond to the evidence and arguments presented in the trial. The composition of the jury, therefore, can go a long way in determining the outcome of a criminal trial.

Supposedly defendants are tried by a jury of their peers. The closest one could realistically come to this ideal would be a jury that at least comprises a representative sampling of the citizenry. But social and economic biases enter into the selection process itself. Since juries are selected from the voter registration rolls, large segments of the population are systematically excluded from jury participation, including political dissenters, lower economic groups, migrants, and the like—precisely those classes of people who most frequently face criminal prosecution (Strodtbeck *et al.*, 1957:713).

Secondly, it is conceivable that, like any group endeavor, the decisions the jury arrives at are not the product of equal participation of all members. Rather, certain individuals dominate and thereby influence the deliberation process. In a series of studies conducted on mock jury deliberations, Strodtbeck and his associates (1957, 1961) imply this conclusion.

Returning to the research carried out by Kalven and Zeisel (1966:488) for the moment, it was argued in this study that in all cases (except for the few hung juries, comprising 5 per cent of the sample) the jury was unanimous in its conclusion. But since there is reason to assume that unanimity is not always present at the start of deliberation, the process must involve some activity in which members of the jury who were initially disposed to a different opinion are persuaded to change their votes. Moreover, it was discovered that in most cases the final verdict was typically decided by the first ballot, so that the deliberation is not a decision-forming process but an implementive process in which some members of the jury convince the dissenters to agree with the dominant view. Who influences whom in the jury room?

Strodtbeck found in his research that certain classes of individuals seem to be highly instrumental in determining the outcome of the deliberation. According to this investigation, jurors tend to stratify themselves along the class and status lines found in the general social structure. Strodtbeck attempted to determine the extent to which each juror participated in the proceedings by recording the amount of time dominated by each juror in the deliberation. It was expected that those who dominated the conversation would be of higher social status. The findings of the study confirmed this expectation. Not only did Strodtbeck find status differentiations in the domination of the conversation; status distinctions were also significant in the selection of foremen. Proprietors and clerical groups tended to rate high on both measures, whereas skilled workers and manual laborers rated low.

It can be reasonably argued that the jury's final decision tends to reflect the attitudes and values of the group dominating the jury room. This is supported by the fact that the more active (high-status) jury participants were less likely to shift their original decisions than the less active (low-status) members, and the latter more frequently altered their opinions in compliance with the dominating group.

In any case, it is apparent that in the jury room at least the law is applied according to the wishes and values of certain segments of the population. In many respects these elements of society act like an interest group not substantially different from the interest groups originally involved in the formation of criminal laws.

Whether or not the wishes of this group are representative of those held by the members of society as a whole is, as yet, undetermined. The jury's verdict may not represent departure from the views and wishes of the wider population at all. Indeed, it probably reflects these views and wishes. Yet, the claim that the jury trial provides the purest example of public opinion in law requires qualification.

GETTING ONE'S DUE: SENTENCING IN CRIMINAL CASES

For a person suspected of criminal activity, the decision to prosecute him is the most crucial step in his confrontation with the judicial machinery. But for the convicted criminal, the most important decision is the sentence he is to receive—the penalty society wishes to impose upon him for his misdeed. Given the liberal use of the negotiated plea of guilty, the sentence a defendant will receive is frequently a foregone conclusion and hardly a surprise. Although defendants may grumble, probably few are dissatisfied with the actual sentence because they tend to measure the penalty received against what they were told they might have gotten had they fought the case and lost (Casper, 1972:92).

To say that the sentence is a foregone conclusion is not, however, quite accurate. Except in those cases where a specific penalty is agreed upon beforehand, plea negotiation can only influence sentencing to a limited extent. It is still the province of the judge to decide what punishment any particular defendant will actually confront. As Kaplan indicates (1973:485), in most jurisdictions and for most crimes the sentencing decision is totally within the realm of the judge. Although his discretion is usually limited by statutory minimum and maximum penalties, in many cases the judge has the option to determine how much of the maximum term the person will receive, when he will be eligible for parole, or whether he will ever see the inside of a prison at all. In this regard, the judge can decide the severity of punishment as well as the type of penalty received. The usual options are imprisonment, probation, fine, or any combination of these, including, of course, the death penalty where it is in effect. A judge can also sentence a person and then suspend the penalty. What is clear is that, like every other decision in the processing of a criminal case, sentencing is a matter involving considerable discretion. For our purposes, the factors affecting the decision-making process for sentencing are of major concern.

Several studies have demonstrated that a great disparity exists between different courts with regard to the sentences given for essentially the same crimes. Some courts appear to be systematically lenient with all classes of offenders while other judges impose comparatively harsh penalties. It is also well known that the average sentences imposed by American criminal courts tend to be somewhat harsher than those levied in many European countries. The United States today has the dubious distinction of putting a larger proportion of its population in prison for longer periods of time than any other country of the Western Hemisphere.

The extent of the disparity in criminal sentences is documented by the findings of several classic studies. In an early investigation focusing on the sentencing practices of six judges in a New Jersey County Court, Frederick Gaudet (1933) reviewed the sentences imposed in over 7,600 cases over a ten-year period. Two judges tended to be consistently more lenient than the others, imprisoning no more than one third of their offenders, while the other judges generally averaged half or more. Judges also varied in the types of crime for which they gave out prison sentences, although no consistent pattern was revealed by the data.

A later study examined 1,437 cases processed by 18 judges in Philadelphia (Green, 1961). The focus of this study was on the legal and nonlegal factors that affect sentencing practices. Legal factors included the number of charges against the defendant, his prior record, the type of crime committed, and the recommendations of other officials. Nonlegal factors were the age, sex, race, and the like of the offender. In general, legal factors explained most of the discrepancies in the sentences imposed by the judges. Among the more important of these were the seriousness of the offense and the previous record of the defendant. Over-all, those offenders whose crimes involved personal injury to a victim were treated most harshly.

In an attempt to measure the sentencing practices of judges confronting similar kinds of cases, Green constructed a prediction table using the legal factors in combination. Employing this table it was possible to determine the likelihood of a person's receiving a long or short sentence or probation. When judges' practices were compared in light of this table it was found that although there appeared to be a high degree of consistency between judges, this varied by degree of seriousness. That is, all judges treated serious offenders in very much the same way. More minor cases, however, reflected the individual opinions of each judge.

Given these and similar findings, the problem for the criminologist is to explain the apparent inconsistencies and discrepancies in sentencing. So far the answers to this question have been less than satisfactory. As Hood and Sparks (1970:152-54) point out, almost all researchers attribute differences in sentencing to individual differences in judges. Although few provide information to support the claim, most studies imply that sentencing policies reflect the "personality" of the judge. Included in this term is reference to the social background, temperament, attitudes, education, religion, political orientation, and the like of the judges.

It is difficult to discern what the investigators really mean by these claims. Hood and Sparks list at least two separate implications. For one, it might be the case that judges do not follow any single consistent policy in sentencing but, rather, make the decision in a completely arbitrary fashion. Or it could be that judges are influenced by factors like race or social-class prejudices, which should not be included in any sentencing decision. The research designed to determine which, if either, of these ideas is correct has not been able to resolve the issue. Yet this is not to imply that it cannot be decided.

A model suggested by Hood and Sparks (1970:156–60) suggests that judges operate so as to classify cases into categories of "typical cases" and make their dispositional decisions according to these categorizations.* To the extent that judges employ different categories of typical cases or employ different factors to make category assignments, one can expect to find differences in sentencing. The problem is to determine the factors judges use to construct and assign persons to various sentencing categories.

Although Hood and Sparks do not carry out their analysis to the extent we might desire, they do suggest some areas of inquiry. As far as the judge himself is concerned, his general view of his work, his attitudes toward crime and punishment, his political orientation, and the like might be important in influencing categorization. These factors may, in turn, be affected by a number of personal and role-related attributes such as the judge's length of experience, his age, and various personality traits.

But no judge is solely influenced by his own attitudes and opinions. He is typically presented with information about the offense and the offender, and recommendations are made as to an appropriate sentence by a number of persons—especially the prosecutor. Judges may, of course, differ on the weight they assign to this information, what kinds of information they choose to pay attention to, whose recommendations they follow, and what data they consider valid. But, as one defendant put it, "The

---

* This observation probably applies to all elements of the legal structure. Note Sudnow's (1965) description of the Public Defender's office for an example.

prosecutor is the fellow that gives you the time" (Casper, 1972: 136). At least the matter deserves much more research than it has up to now received.

THE JUVENILE COURT

On July 1, 1899, a new concept in the administration of criminal justice received formal recognition when the first juvenile court in the world began its legal existence in Chicago, Illinois. The law creating this court altered the status of children in Western society and revolutionized the judicial procedures designed to handle this class of persons. Misbehaving children could no longer be considered or treated as criminals but became wards of the state who were in need of care, protection, or discipline. Children, thus, were not to be punished for their misdeeds but rehabilitated and salvaged to become useful, productive, law-abiding adults. By 1945 all states in the union had adopted laws of this kind, and the philosophy underlying juvenile justice has continued to find increasing adoption throughout the world (Caldwell, 1961).

Today over 3,000 juvenile courts exist in the United States alone. All these courts have jurisdiction over delinquency cases, and a majority deal with cases involving dependency and neglect as well. Frequently the distinction among the three is hard to discern. Officially a delinquent is defined as an individual below a certain designated age who committed an act that if committed by an adult would be considered a crime. But delinquency statutes are characteristically broader than this, including in their provision a hodgepodge of youthful problems like truancy, waywardness, incorrigibility, association with immoral persons, and the like (cf. Kittrie, 1973:119). It is indeed a truism that a juvenile can be apprehended and incarcerated merely for standing in front of a pool hall. Children who are dependent or neglected are usually dealt with by the court as "Persons in need of supervision" (PINS), and some cases of delinquency can also be handled in these terms.

Since juveniles are not considered criminals, a new set of procedures with corresponding terminology had to be adopted to hear cases involving juveniles. The key features of the juvenile court are informality in proceedings and individualization of justice (treatment). Moreover, since the court is supposed to be informal, rules of evidence are relaxed, and standards of proof are lowered. Given that the supposed concern of the court is the welfare and protection of the child, as opposed to his punishment, these seem, at first glance, to be reasonable and probably desirable measures. Indeed, most people at first were enthusiastic about the juvenile court idea. Few expressed much concern that the court's informal procedures might permit violation of the individual's due-process rights. As time progressed, however, a number of people became alarmed over the inequities and injustices practiced by juvenile courts. A growing number of individuals have voiced considerable disappointment with and criticism of the operation of juvenile justice. Those objections center primarily on the denial of legal rights for juveniles.

The formation of the juvenile court is significant for two reasons. One, it represents a philosophical position that has found increasing acceptance and implementation throughout the entire judicial and penal realm. Yet it is precisely this philosophy that underlies many of the abuses sensitive scholars and jurists have found most reprehensible. Second, the juvenile court's formation marks a significant change in legal standards and the treatment of offenders. Grounded in the ideology of therapy, questions of guilt become, if not irrelevant to judicial proceedings, at least secondary to the goal of rehabilitation.

The origins of the juvenile court have been traced to the concept of *parens patriae* (the idea that the king, as the father of his country, could exercise guardianship over minors), which was administered through the courts of equity in medieval England (cf. Kittrie, 1973:4–11). The actual development of the juvenile court was given impetus by the child-welfare movements and growth of the social-welfare mentality of the late nineteenth century. But, as ultimately formulated, the entire concept of juvenile delinquency is based on a social-scientific image of the delinquent. Although it is of dubious validity, this image sees delinquency as

. . . symptomatic of some underlying emotional condition which must be diagnosed by means of the concepts and techniques of psychiatry, psychology, and social work, and for which treatment, not punishment, must be administered through the efforts of a team of psychiatrists, psychologists, and social workers [Caldwell, 1961:496].

In effect, delinquent children are considered "sick" in some way. Hence, they are to be "cured" and returned to the community. Even if one were to grant that the sickness analogy has merit, this premise still assumes that the causes underlying the illness are known and, even more, how to cure them.

The concept that delinquents as such are sick is frightful enough in itself, bringing to mind images of a *Clockwork Orange* kind of world. But in order for the rehabilitative philosophy underlying the formation of the juvenile court to be carried out in practice, significant alterations had to take place in the machinery designed to select those persons "in need of treatment"/ from those not so afflicted. The procedures unique to the juvenile court are supposedly designed to make this determination while at the same time protecting the child from the trauma and stigma of criminal proceedings.

The cornerstone of the ideology, if not of the actual practice, of adult criminal courts is the procedural rules of due process. The whole intent of these rules is to protect the individual from the erroneous and arbitrary repression administered by the state in criminal cases. But if the accused is considered a ward of the state, and if the concern is with treatment and individualized justice, it follows that any procedures that might block the effective implementation of these goals must be swept aside. Due-process rules are just this kind of stumbling block.

After all, since delinquency is not considered the same as crime, and since the proceedings in juvenile cases are regarded as civil as opposed to criminal in nature, the constitutional rights of due process do not apply to the juvenile court. In fact, as Caldwell and others have observed, the philosophy of juvenile justice presupposes a negation of due process in principle. It is the child's welfare, not his guilt, that is at issue. Hence, the judge must be granted broad powers to decide the fate of those brought before him. Playing the role of loving parent, benevolently concerned for the well-being of the child, the judge is supposed to be concerned not only with what the child *did* but with what he *is* (Kittrie, 1973:111–17). Rules of evidence and standards of proof basic to criminal courts can only hamper the judge in fulfilling his obligation. Some have even argued that procedures governed by the standards for the criminal court could only be harmful to the juvenile.

The concept of juvenile justice still holds great appeal for many people and it is not likely to be abolished in the near future. The questions raised by opponents have, however, received increasing attention. Three major issues still plague the juvenile court. As listed by Caldwell (1961), these include the court's effectiveness, its jurisdiction, and the legality of its procedures. It is still not clear just where the problem lies. That is, are the difficulties plaguing the court today merely a personnel problem or a more basic issue stemming from the very philosophical premises of the court?

The evidence is clear that trained, skilled, and kindly people are not always available to act in the capacity of juvenile judges. Nor are special facilities and staff with the necessary knowledge and skill to deal with delinquents in sufficient supply (cf. McCune and Skoler, 1965; Walther and McCune, 1965). But it is still an open question as to whether adequate facilities and personnel would improve the court or increase its effectiveness.

Possibly the problem is deeper than administrative considerations. Despite arguments to the contrary, the delinquency label is just as onerous as the criminal designation, and the disposition of a delinquent case infringes on the freedom and rights of the individual as much as does any criminal sentence. Also, it has become apparent to many that a number of juveniles have been treated in an unfair and arbitrary manner by the court designed to protect them. Tappan (1949:208) has said that if the juvenile court is to act as the savior of the child, the problem still remains as to who is to save the child from his savior. This has become increasingly cogent as more and more is learned about the operation of juvenile justice.

The Gault case illustrates these points nicely (see Kittrie, 1973:122, 138n). Gerald Gault, at the time of his sentencing, was a 15-year-old boy accused of having made an obscene phone call. He was found guilty by a juvenile court in Arizona and committed to an institution for six years. The offense would have been a misdemeanor had it been committed by an adult. At his hearing, Gault had no lawyer, no prior notice had been given to his parents concerning the charges against him, there was no sworn testimony, and Gault had been required to incriminate himself. The Supreme Court's ruling in this case, reversing the lower court, stands as a landmark decision for reform. In this decision the Court sought to extend to juveniles many of the rights accorded adult defendants in criminal cases by ruling that juveniles had the right to be informed of the charges against them, to be represented by an attorney, to confront and cross-examine witnesses, to be protected from self-incrimination, to be provided with a transcript of the proceedings, and to appeal.

This decision was given further weight by the recommendations of the President's Commission on Law Enforcement and Administration of Justice (1967:84–88). The Commission advocated that (1) legal counsel be allowed for all juveniles facing delinquency charges, (2) evidence be restricted to legally admissible kinds, at least at the adjudication stage, (3) reforms be instituted in the areas of notice, detention, and confidentiality of records, and, possibly most significant, (4) hearings be divided into adjudication and dispositional phases. The adjudication stage would concern itself solely with the guilt or innocence of the child, following procedures similar to those used in criminal cases. The dispositional phase, in conformity with the philosophy underlying the juvenile court, could be less formal and directed to the most appropriate disposition of those individuals found guilty of delinquent behavior.

Implementation of these measures is likely to be slow at best. Nor are the controversies surrounding the juvenile court likely to subside. But the conclusion that the court could stand a dose of reform is rarely disputed. A society with a large and increasing population of juveniles, a society that cherishes freedom and the rights of the individual, a society that is truly concerned with the welfare of its members would be hypocritical if it subjected a large portion of its population to a judicial system that has shown itself to be largely unconcerned about their freedom, rights, or welfare.

CREATING THE CRIMINAL: A COMMENTARY

Criminal sanctions are supposedly directed toward a person's behavior—what he does, not what kind of person he is. Yet, the research on the administration of criminal justice reported in this chapter, however limited that discussion might be, reveals that just the opposite occurs. A person is likely to acquire a social identity as a criminal precisely because of what he is—because of the kind of personal or social characteristics he has the misfortune to possess. Being black, poor, migrant, uneducated, and the like increases a person's chances of being defined as a criminal. The special case of juvenile delinquency is but an extreme example of a mentality that is pervasive throughout the entire system of criminal justice. For example, Kittrie (1973:111) quotes the statement of a leading juvenile-court judge who suggested:

> The problem for determination [in juvenile-court hearings] is not, "Has this boy or girl committed a specific wrong," but "What is he, how has he become what he is, and what had best be done in his interest and in the interest of the state to save him from a downward career?"

Even though it is behavior that is subject to regulation by the law, when one looks at the workings of law-enforcement agencies one finds that behavior actually serves to provide an excuse for transforming a preformed judgment of a person into a socially sanctioned reality.

It is not so much that American criminal courts are unjust, although they surely are. Nor is the issue the fact that court procedures are arbitrary and discriminatory; any defendant knows that. Many of the problems alluded to in this chapter are essentially technical in nature and easily remedied. What I am suggesting here is that the very structure and operation of the judicial system, which was created to deal with the problem called crime, are not only grounded in an unstated image of the criminal but also—merely because the system exists—serve to produce and perpetuate the "thing" it was created to handle. That is to say, the criminal court (and especially the juvenile court) does not exist in its present form because the people it deals with are what they are. Rather, the criminals and delinquents become the way they are characterized by others as being because the court (and the world view it embodies) exists in the form that it does. *The criminal, thus, is a "product" of the structural and procedural characteristics of the judicial system.*

Throughout this discussion, we have seen that specific criminal cases tend to be handled in perfunctory, routine ways. The suggestion was made that individuals coming before the court are placed into categoric stereotypes, which separate the respectable noncriminal elements from the criminal ones. The respectables are quickly discharged while the criminals are rapidly processed. Bureaucratic and personal factors were cited as responsible in large part for judicial action. If this procedure generates something less than criminal justice, we should not be at all surprised. The system is simply not designed to dispense "justice." It is designed to get results, and "results" means conviction or officially defined criminals. Thus the court functions to confirm the reality of which its very existence is a reflection. Would it make any sense to have a judicial system had it not been decided beforehand that certain kinds of people exist to be processed by that system? Furthermore, could this institution endure if it did not operate so as to validate the kind of world its very presence presupposes?

As we saw in our critique of etiology, crime can be produced as a social reality because members of society are able to conceive of a physical entity called a criminal. To do so requires that members construct the criminal as a specific type of person. It follows that crime does exist because we can and do locate examples of this type of person in the world. The judicial system is but a set of methods and procedures designed and historically perfected to transform a conceptual reality into a social reality. The system and the form that it takes are, therefore, contingent on the image (mental reality) that members hold of the world and the possible kinds of people who populate it. As that image or conception changes over time, the legal institution built upon it likewise changes, but more slowly. (This is clearly seen in the growth of the therapeutic state and the ideology of rehabilitation.) In the end, the physical world, like the social world, is a product of our minds—our mental reality. The world, that is, is the world members create in terms of the world they perceive to exist.

That criminal courts are arbitrary and discriminatory should also occasion no surprise. Judicial authorities are not immune to common-sense conceptions of the world. Since society employs these individuals to do its dirty work, it is likely that they would adhere to society's wishes, or to what they perceive those wishes to be. In any case, they serve to confirm reality experiences. It is their *raison d'être* to sort out the bad from the good, the degradable from the normal, the criminal from the noncriminal. By doing so judicial authorities do more than simply sustain the status quo. They do more than verify members' reality conceptions. They also confirm our images of ourselves as righteous, normal, law-abiding citizens (Lofland, 1969:305; Douglas, 1970:3).

Civil libertarians may lament judicial authorities' failure to follow the rules of the game. In this they are obviously correct. But they are countered by the conservative repressives who claim that the legal institution was created to protect us and that the courts are frustrated in achieving this goal by overrestrictive rules of procedure. In fact, due process and crime control are not competing and opposing philosophical positions but merely disagreements over how the game is to be played. Few have yet objected to the game per se. The alternatives, however, are limited only by our imaginations (cf. Quinney, 1972; 1973).

6

Criminal Corrections: The Nature and Impact of Societal Reaction

CRIMINALIZATION DOES NOT SIMPLY END once a person has been pronounced guilty of a criminal offense. As Austin Turk (1969:18) points out, an analysis of the criminalization process is, in effect, an analysis of the sanctioning process. Accordingly, "criminality is . . . the state of having been officially defined as punishable, whether or not one has been apprehended and punished." In this sense, criminal punishment is a form of official coercion that results in deprivation. This deprivation may be permanent or temporary. It can take a number of forms, including incarceration, material deprivation, status loss, and attempts at rehabilitation. In short, a person encounters punishment when and if societal members react to his conduct by depriving him of something he values—his liberty, wealth, identity, or a second chance.

Even though it can be said that a person is being formally subjected to punishment as early in the legal process as the stage of investigation or apprehension, the infliction of punishment officially falls within the duties of criminal corrections. Sociologists have long been interested in the correctional institution. In fact, the science of penology is devoted exclusively to studying the various kinds of correctional programs that deal with individuals defined as "criminal." It is beyond the scope of this book to discuss these programs in detail, but this chapter endeavors to analyze the nature, grounds, and impact of correctional programs in general.

CORRECTIONAL PROGRAMS

The President's Commission on Law Enforcement and Administration of Justice (1967:161) reports that on any given day over one and a quarter million persons are being formally "corrected" for criminal offenses in the United States alone. Roughly 426,000 (or 35 per cent) of these individuals are incarcerated in some kind of institution. The rest are either on probation, released on parole, or free in the community on other grounds (e.g., free on appeal, released after payment of a fine, involved in some rehabilitation program). Considering that more than eight million people are arrested every year for criminal offenses, more than two and a quarter million of them charged with serious crimes, it is obvious that only a small percentage of lawbreakers ever actually experience the full impact of criminal sanctions.

There is much disparity in the kind and severity of treatment received by those individuals who are subjected to correctional activity. Juvenile delinquents, for example, are more frequently dealt with by probation; over 65 per cent of those adjudicated as delinquent receive this disposition. Adult felons, on the other hand, are more likely to be incarcerated, although even here the majority are outside prison walls. Imprisonment is usually reserved for offenders who are thought to be most criminalistic in character and, thus, less likely to refrain from further illegal conduct. This group includes serious violators, repeaters, and members of minority groups.

More than 120,000 employees work for the correctional system in various capacities (President's Commission on Law Enforcement and Administration of Justice, 1967:159–85). These employees handle approximately 1,300,000 offenders daily. Thus the ratio of correctors to correctees is 1:10. Fewer than 20 per cent of these officials are engaged in rehabilitation activities (using that term loosely), so that, on the average, there is one rehabilitation worker for every 54 offenders. In contrast, over 80 per cent of the correctional employees are concerned primarily with guarding inmates. That's one guard for every 14 offenders.

Table 3 shows that for the 285,000 (per day) juvenile delinquents on probation, over 87 per cent are supervised by probation officers responsible for overseeing 50 "clients" or more. Over 50 per cent of all juvenile probationers are part of caseloads numbering 70 or more clients. If a probation officer were to see at least one client per day, on the average, in a 20-day month he could see each client once every three months. Adult offenders receive even less supervision, since approximately 88 per cent (felony cases only) are in caseloads numbering 70 or more clients, and some 76 per cent are "supervised" by probation officers with at least 100 clients. Other "treatment" services are even scarcer. For example, psychiatric services are so infrequent in prisons that if all convicts were to receive equal amounts of counseling, each would get 82 seconds of therapy per month (Schnur, 1958).

TABLE 3

Caseloads Supervised by Probation Officers

	Caseload Size			
	0–50 Clients	51–70 Clients	71–100 Clients	100-plus Clients
Juvenile	11.76%	31.15%	46.41%	10.68%
Misdemeanant	.86	8.12	14.68	76.34
Adult Felon	3.10	9.16	20.69	67.05

SOURCE: Adapted from President's Commission on Law Enforcement and Administration of Justice, 1967:168-69.

Even though a good deal of verbiage has been expended on the new penology, and even though some efforts have been made to implement the philosophy of rehabilitation, these figures alone indicate that the establishment of full-fledged programs of correctional therapy is not even close to being realized for criminal offenders. Yet, a sizable number of people are processed by the correctional apparatus every year. Rehabilitation is frequently cited as the chief goal of this activity. Criminals, it is said, are no longer punished; they are to be changed in some way so as to deter them from their sinful ways. The role of criminology in this "new penology," in part, is to analyze the success correctional officials have had in accomplishing this goal and the alternatives available for increasing that success.

What happens to the individuals who are subjected to criminal corrections? To what extent are the various correctional programs successful? What accounts for their success or failure? Indeed, what constitutes success for criminal corrections? What are the alternatives? Seeking answers to these and related issues is the main concern of the rest of this chapter.

THE HISTORY OF PUNISHMENT: AN OVERVIEW*

Historically, criminal correction has experienced three overlapping developmental stages. Until the twelfth century, crime was considered a highly individual matter to be resolved by either blood feud or the payment of compensation to the injured party. But no formal machinery was in existence to enforce this policy.

It was only when the state in the person of the king began to assume control over criminal justice that the system of corrections that has evolved to the present time began to emerge. Once crime was defined as an offense against the state, the state, rather than the individual harmed, became the avenger. The practice of inflicting punishment in the form of pain became the standard response to crime.

Throughout this period, criminal offenders were subjected to execution for a wide range of activities, many of which are considered trivial today. Violators were also made to undergo a variety of forms of physical torture, although the use of torture varied from time to time, being either an end in itself or a means to extract confessions of wrongdoing. Branding, disfigurement, dismemberment, and other physical abuses have been used systematically to punish those who break the criminal law.

Along with corporal punishment, banishment was and has remained a characteristic response to violations of criminal laws. In fact, banishment is probably the purest expression of deviance identification. Since to be defined as a criminal (deviant) is to be designated as a nonmember, an outsider, banishing a person from society symbolically reveals that person's nonmember status for all to see.

---

* For more extensive discussions consult Gibbons (1968:435-42), Sutherland and Cressey (1966:305-64), and Barnes and Teeters (1959:285-347). Also see Sellin (1958) and American Correctional Association (1972).

The forms of banishment range from the extremes of execution (banishment to another world) to the common practices of shunning or snubbing. In criminal cases, banishment has usually involved deportation or transportation. The populations of several American colonies, Australia, and New Zealand at one time consisted largely of criminals "transported" to these places to work as slaves or indentured servants. Today these forms of banishment have been replaced by imprisonment and other types of institutionalization.

Before the end of the eighteenth century, the contemporary idea that criminals should be incarcerated for long periods of time in some facility exclusively designed for that purpose was foreign to the human mind. That convicts were to be changed while retained in these facilities is a notion that did not emerge until considerably later.

It is obvious that in these early responses to criminal offenders the idea of rehabilitating and reinstating the criminal to full participation rights was not the principal goal. Whereas corporal punishment reflects society's hatred of the criminal, the practice of banishment reveals the fear societal members have of lawbreakers. In any case, early forms of correctional response were directed to incapacitating the offender in the hope of gaining some protection for society by keeping the criminal at bay. Possibly some rudimentary notion of deterrence was also involved. And revenge, retaliation, and retribution were surely underlying considerations, as they are today. As we shall see, the largely contradictory objectives required of correctional personnel are among the main factors frustrating the successful accomplishments of any particular goal they might seek to fulfill.

At least during the Middle Ages, when corporal punishment was at its height, the implementation of criminal justice was swift and sure. Since the concept of imprisonment as a correctional technique had not emerged, early jails were but temporary housing facilities for individuals destined for the stake, the block, or the gallows. The forerunners of the modern prison can be traced to the poorhouses (houses of correction) established in sixteenth-century England. But the concept of imprisonment as a form of punishment did not emerge until the eighteenth century in America. The first prison to be opened was Philadelphia's Walnut Street Jail—ironically, in 1776. By 1829 a second prison of this type was opened at Cherry Hill, Pennsylvania. A prison system came into being.

The Pennsylvania prison system was based on the concept of solitary confinement. Prisoners were locked in individual cells, given a Bible to read, and told to do penance and reform their evil ways. It is instructive to note the religious overtones of these early prisons, the term penitentiary deriving as it does from the same root as the word *repent*.

New York State followed Pennsylvania, introducing its prison system at Auburn in 1819. This was followed by the famous Sing Sing prison, built at Ossining a few years later. The New York system was based on a congregate organization wherein prisoners mingled with one another inside the prison walls to engage in a variety of tasks. Since prisoners were expected to work to earn their keep and, if possible, show a profit for the prison, it is not unwarranted to say that the capitalistic spirit lay behind the founding of American prisons.

Eventually the New York system came to dominate in America while the Pennsylvania system is popular in Europe. Almost all the institutions constructed in the United States since the 1800s follow the Auburn–Sing Sing model. The high walls, gun towers, tiers of barred cells, and the like, which form the essential architectural features of these institutions, are familiar to anyone acquainted with old films. It is only lately that alternative designs have been used more extensively, especially in California, where the wall has been replaced by chain link fences, and the tiers of cells with cottages or large dormitory-like structures.

With the growth of the imprisonment idea, banishment came to be seen as a more or less temporary necessity for rehabilitation rather than a goal to be sought. With the rise of humanitarian ideals, permanent banishment became offensive and is rarely practiced in modern Western society today (except for aliens). The goal has become that of restoring the violator to "wholeness," to the extent possible. As a result, the morally deviant, such as the evil, the insane, the bad, the bizarre, and the criminal, are supposedly "treated" and, if possible, rehabilitated rather than merely punished. Yet, in order to accomplish this, banishment, at least in a temporary form, is still practiced, adding the problem

of how to rehabilitate inmates while at the same time retaining
them in some kind of facility in the already overburdened correctional system.

REHABILITATION VS. PUNISHMENT

The idea of rehabilitation is a relatively new phenomenon in
human history, although, in practice, some forms of rehabilitative
behavior are characteristic of all social groups. For example, the
practice of instructing or teaching the young the correct or appropriate way to do something involves correctional activity. The
practice of snubbing those who act in offensive ways (which is
carried out in most human groups) is also a form of rehabilitating
activity. In both cases, some course of action is engaged in by
some group in order to bring a dissenting member into line. The
germ of the rehabilitation ideology is contained in the phrase
"bringing into line." The modern concept of rehabilitation has
refined this general idea to a considerable extent. As Robert
Straus (n.d.:1) points out, the term rehabilitation is applied to a
broad range of disabling human problems, from physical disabil-
ity to mental illness. Its application to crime and delinquency
is one of the more recent extensions.

In the simplest sense, rehabilitation consists of some course of
action directed to transforming individuals into less undesirable,
more complete and adequate, better-functioning social beings. As
far as criminal correction is concerned, the minimal aim is to
make lawbreakers into law-abiders. In short, rehabilitation is an
attempt to restore discredited individuals to the status of full-
fledged, participating members of society. In this sense, the concept is revolutionary.

With the development of this idea a fundamental shift occurred in the conception of the criminal. Prior to this time criminals were considered "bad" or "evil." Hence, they were to be
punished merely because of their "badness." Now, however, the
criminal is more and more seen as "sick" in one way or another.
Thus, criminals are no more to be punished for their conduct
than someone suffering from a common cold. Instead criminals are to be "treated" in order to cure them of their sickness
and make them emotionally healthy, law-abiding citizens—just
like the rest of us.

The treatment model used by criminal corrections draws its operative approach from medical science and its philosophical underpinnings from humanism. Human engineering in general and criminal rehabilitation in particular grew out of a union between the ideals of humanism and the teachings of psychoanalysis and psychological behaviorism. This development is probably one of the more important and potentially dangerous events of the recent century.

Many of the people who argue that correctional programs should be basically rehabilitative rather than punitive in nature consider rehabilitation to be not an alternative to pure punishment but fundamentally different from punishment. But as it is practiced today, punishment has actually been largely redefined and justified as a form of rehabilitation. Criminals, after all, are not punished any more for purely expressive reasons. Punishment carried out in a humane way (if that is possible) and in the name of rehabilitation is not punishment but a deterrent. At least that is what some people would say.

But this misses the point. The goal of rehabilitation is to resocialize offenders by building into them the motivation to obey the law. To misconstrue rehabilitation as being fundamentally different from punishment only serves to frustrate the successful implementation of rehabilitative programs. For if rehabilitation seeks to deflect individuals from engaging in further illegal activity, it really makes little difference whether this is accomplished by means of psychotherapy, incarceration, or physical brutality. The goal sought by rehabilitation programs does not, that is, differ from the one supposedly pursued by punitive plans. Only the means of achieving the goal differ. In the end, the attitude societal members harbor toward the criminal (besides the goal sought in correcting him) are the same anyway—the criminal cannot be allowed to remain the kind of person he has been defined as being.

In a number of writings, Don Gibbons (cf. 1968) has clearly described the overriding similarities between punishment and rehabilitation. Primarily, as Gibbons notes, both stem from a common pragmatic principle, if not an identical philosophical base. Punishment, to be sure, was systematically practiced long before a clear-cut philosophy or goal was created to justify it.

The justifications that were eventually formulated were couched in terms of the prevailing commonsense images people held of the criminal. The first major efforts along these lines are found in the writings of the classical school of criminology. As we discussed in Chapter 3, this school postulated a rational-man conception of the offender. The criminal deliberately chooses to do wrong for the purpose of achieving pleasure. Logically, then, the affliction of pain in the form of punishment should serve to deter him from his errant ways. The idea of deterrence, thus, came to stand as the central logical premise for all forms of punishment practiced in the name of justice. But punishment has been justified on other grounds as well (cf. Tappan, 1960; Handerich, 1971; Packer, 1968:31–61).

One goal commonly sought in the pursuit of punishment is the basic desire to *retaliate* against those who have injured us, to inflict harm on those who have inflicted harm on us. In the same sense, *retribution* has frequently been stated as an objective of punishment. Where retaliation is directed toward the offender in order to cause him injury for injury received, retribution is geared to receiving from the offender some sense of restoration or compensation for loss. If a person is murdered he cannot, of course, be compensated for his loss. But some social balance can be realized by executing the murderer.

Finally, if a person cannot be prevented from violating social laws, society can at least make it more difficult for him to do so again. That is, the person can be *incapacitated* so that he is prevented from misbehaving, at least during the time he is being punished. The original goal of corrections remains, but now it is supported by other rationales. Incapacitation has also become refined. If nothing else, imprisonment serves to prevent rule breakers from harming decent folk during their term of institutionalization. Apparently, though, it does little to prevent them from harming one another.

Incapacitation can probably best be understood as one form of deterrent. According to classical and neo-classical thought, punishment is to be employed as a specific deterrent to individual lawbreakers. The threat of punishment should, it is believed, operate in a similar way as incapacitation to stop an individual who may be contemplating criminal activity from carrying his thoughts through to completion. The experience of having been punished, moreover, is supposed to prevent the offender from contemplating crime again.

But the advocates of rehabilitation argue that offenders can be deterred from crime in another way, that they can be changed in some way or another so as to block their deviant impulses. To do so, it is argued, the individuals' psyches must be altered, or their attitudes modified, or they need to be provided with job skills, or whatever. These practices, it is thought, are not only more effective but at the same time more humane.

All treatment and rehabilitation efforts rest on the premise that deviant kinds of behavior stem from some particular set of factors or conditions that propel or draw individuals into misconduct. In order to prevent individuals from engaging in this conduct these factors must be diagnosed and then altered or eliminated. Eliminating these conditions is the essence of rehabilitation work. Of necessity, this work requires that the person afflicted be changed in some way.

On the surface this appears reasonable. But rehabilitation is based on the assumption that criminals are to some extent rational, free agents with some control over their own actions. They may have encountered social liabilities that make it more difficult for them to adhere to the law than others, but they still have law-abiding options open to them. The trouble lies in the person's ability (or lack of ability) to cope with his limitations and handicaps. Hence, the task of rehabilitating criminals is essentially to motivate them in some way to abide by the law.

This line of thought bears striking similarities to the philosophy underlying punishment. While classical writers attributed criminal conduct to one factor, pleasure seeking, rehabilitation advocates have done little more than integrate this notion into a broader theory of human behavior. Crime is still defined as the product of pernicious motivation. All that has been changed is that now we are given explanations of the source of these motivations or why individuals are unable to surmount them. Punishment is disparaged then only because it is the wrong tactic, not because it is objectionable in its own right.

REHABILITATION VS. HUMANITARIANISM

In the view of many individuals, rehabilitative programs are nothing more than ways of avoiding "just" punishment. Some people argue that rehabilitation is tantamount to coddling criminals, making it desirable to engage in socially offensive activity. Others tend to confuse humanitarian gestures with treatment. Proponents of this view advocate tennis courts in prisons, remedial-reading programs, leather shops, and the like in the hope that these programs will serve to "cure" criminals of their antisocial ways.

Both views are naïve because they rest on equally misguided (though different) ideas about the nature and goals of rehabilitation. The first argument suggests that rehabilitative activities are somewhat less than painful. But convicts don't seem to agree. Most would probably prefer to be left alone to do their time. The second argument is erroneous because it assumes that humane treatment will automatically lead an individual to reform his ways. This is not only untrue but also potentially self-defeating.

When people speak of rehabilitation in humanistic terms they usually refer to things like providing the offender with adequate food and clothing, reasonably comfortable surroundings, work and recreational opportunities, some contact with friends and relatives, and the like (Gibbons, n.d.). From the perspective of rehabilitation, however, these humanitarian gestures have no more relation to treatment than a doctor's bedside manner has to the medication prescribed. To have a congenial doctor may make taking one's medicine a little easier, but the doctor's personality will surely not *heal* a broken leg. If humane gestures contribute to rehabilitation, one would have to assume that the reverse of these conditions are the generating factors behind criminality. That is, one would have to be ready to demonstrate that individuals become criminals because they have inadequate diets, lacked job skills, or have insufficient access to recreational facilities. It is doubtful that this theory can be supported. Nor has it yet been shown that improved diets and the like have any impact on the subsequent behavior of criminals. Being humane to convicts is not, in short, any guarantee that they will mend their ways.

Which is not to say that our social outcasts should not be treated humanely. Humane treatment can and should be defended, but on its own grounds and for its own sake. Convicts should, that is, be treated humanely because there is no reason to do otherwise. We should also not be surprised or enraged if they neglect to thank us for our kindness. Humanitarianism should be practiced because we are humane people. If we were to do otherwise, would we be any different from or better than those we condemn as criminals?

THE IMPACT OF CORRECTIONS

Whatever the ideal of successful rehabilitation might be, it, at minimum, involves some notion of deterrence. It would be exceedingly difficult, if not impossible, to determine the extent to which correctional programs act as a general deterrent for the population at large, although a number of efforts have been made to do this. Calculating the exact number of criminal offenses actually committed has so far been less than satisfactory. Arriving at accurate estimates of how many crimes would have been committed were the threat of punishment not hanging over citizens' heads defies serious contemplation.

For known offenders (convicted criminals) the problem is different, but only slightly less difficult. Typically researchers use some measures of recidivism (reinvolvement in crime) to evaluate the relative merit of various correctional tactics. This measure, while in common use, suffers from a number of defects (Schnur, 1958a). First, it poses technical difficulties. For example, it has yet to be decided what is the best measure of recidivism to use. Also, the time lag and sample loss characteristic of long-term follow-up studies afflict all inquiries of this kind. And the difficulty of determining whether or not individuals who do not acquire rearrest or conviction records have actually remained free from reinvolvement altogether or have just not been caught at it has not been surmounted.

These difficulties aside, the researcher still faces a number of problems in assessing correctional programs. Besides the very basic problem of deciding just what rehabilitation consists of, one still has to determine "the degree to which offenders actually improved as a consequence of the treatment received beyond what would have occurred had no treatment been given in the first place" (Gibbons, n.d.). Secondly, any conclusions one might make regarding success or failure depend on his starting assumptions. If one assumes that all offenders would become reinvolved in crime were nothing done to stop them, then any improvement on total recidivism (any figure lower than 100 per cent) could be called success. On the other hand, it could be assumed that corrections operate on a 100 per cent success basis. If so, anything less than this would be failure. Finally, one could be equivocal about the issue and say that the chances of reinvolvement are 50-50. This being the case, any improvement on a 50 per cent success/failure rate would indicate success.

So far these problems have been dealt with in less than a satisfactory manner. Nor are the data on recidivism all we might like them to be. Consequently, the information and conclusions presented below should be read with several grains of salt. With these precautions in mind, what does the evidence show regarding the impact of conventional corrections?

Interestingly, the bulk of the evidence regarding the deterrent effect of criminal sanctions suggests that the threat of punishment has little impact on potential lawbreakers. Although the issue of deterrence is still being debated (see, e.g., Tittle and Logan, 1972), most individuals who break the law (and get caught) report that the possible consequences of their activity had very little deterring influence on their decision. If anything, the threat of prison forced them to take greater pains in planning their crimes so as not to be caught. With the possible exception of professional or career criminals or those whose crimes required some planning and contemplation, most offenders report that there was little calculation regarding the likelihood of being apprehended *before* they committed their acts. The crime took place, and it was only *after the fact* that they worried about the possibility of being apprehended.

This does not mean that the prospect of a long stretch in prison does not function in a more general way to deter the public at large. Yet, even here, the severity of the sanction appears to make little difference in its deterrent potential. Numerous studies (cf. Schuessler, 1952) show that the death penalty, for example, has only slight deterrent effect on the incidence of murder. For most people, the loss of reputation and social standing is probably quite enough to deter them from crime. Some citizens probably refrain from crime because they find it morally offensive to commit acts that are socially obnoxious and legally prohibited. In any case, imprisonment or other punishment is unnecessary to deter most people from crime, although it is probably the case that the *threat* of punishment is necessary to deter some individuals from wrongdoing. What about those who have actually experienced punishment? Does the experience block them from further involvement in crime?

Most of those convicted of crime are either put in prison or placed on probation, with probation getting the lion's share of the total. Probation, considered the milder form of punishment and the one with the greatest potential for rehabilitation, is, understandably, granted to the younger, less serious, more-likely-to-succeed kinds of offenders. One might expect, therefore, that probationers would exhibit low rates of recidivism.

A good deal of disparity exists in the data, but studies show that roughly 75 per cent of the individuals placed on probation refrain from further criminality. Many of the people who are rearrested, or who have their probation revoked, are technical violators—individuals who break one or another condition of their probation—for example, entering a bar. This research suggests that further criminality is not always the reason behind recidivism. Of those individuals who do experience reconvictions, either during their probationary period or following release, most apparently engage in relatively mild forms of criminality.

For instance, a study by Ralph England (1955) found that of 490 federal offenders released from probation between 1939 and 1944, less than 18 per cent experienced reconviction. Over half of these reconvictions took place in the first three years after release, and approximately 60 per cent were for a variety of offenses including gambling, disorderly conduct, liquor-law violations, larceny, and a few burglary cases.

As for adults released from prisons, the picture, strangely enough, is not altogether different. In an early study, Zuckerman *et al.* (1953) traced the postrelease careers of the 345 inmates released from the Minnesota State Reformatory between 1944 and 1945. Fewer than 50 per cent succeeded in avoiding a legal record in a five-year period. But only 21.2 per cent were actually convicted and recommitted to prison on felony charges. Roughly 2 per cent were readmitted because of parole violations, and twenty individuals (5.8 per cent) were convicted of misdemeanors.

One of the most sophisticated investigations of postrelease success is Daniel Glaser's (1964) massive study of the federal prison and parole system. This study, based on a review of the records of over 1,000 men released from the federal prison system in 1956, reveals that less than one-third of the ex-convicts were reimprisoned within the first five years of release. This, of course, does not mean that the remaining two-thirds stayed "clean" or free from arrest. And, as might be expected, a good deal of variation was found in the rate of reinvolvment by region and type of offender.

Yet, even though a good deal of variation exists, the overall one-third recidivism rate appears to be a reasonably standard figure. It may very well be the case that a large percentage of the individuals incarcerated had experienced imprisonment at some earlier time. This is because ex-cons are more likely to be put in prison should they be rearrested and convicted, not because they are especially prone to committing crime. On the whole the evidence is clear: ex-cons are not the depraved, antisocial, hardened criminals they are often portrayed to be. Hood and Sparks (1970: 186–91) summarize the findings with regard to adult corrections as follows:

1. For many offenders, probation is likely to be at least as effective in preventing recidivism as an institutional sentence. . . .
2. Fines and discharges are much more effective than either probation or imprisonment for first offenders and recidivists of all age groups. . . .
3. Long prison sentences are no more effective in preventing recidivism than shorter ones. . . .
4. The offenders most likely to improve are the "medium risks."

Regarding the last point, Hood and Sparks suggest that persons with a low probability of reinvolvement probably should not be subjected to rehabilitation programs since they apparently don't need them anyway and are not likely to receive any benefit from them if imposed. On the other hand, individuals with a high probability of reinvolvement tend not to benefit from treatment either, no matter what its form, since they are likely to become recidivists no matter what is done for them. Subjecting these individuals to incarceration, psychotherapy, job training, or whatever would make no difference, Hood and Sparks imply. Apparently it would be better to allocate the available resources so as to maximize the amount of rehabilitation given to those who might benefit from it.

When one turns to juvenile institutions, the recidivism picture is quite different. Failure rates for youthful offenders tend to range considerably, being as low as 20 per cent for female delinquents and as high as 70 per cent for male offenders. Reiss (1951: 200) reports, for example, that 32.7 per cent of the boys placed on probation in one study were convicted of violations during their probationary period. Other studies show rates as low as 15 per cent in the case of probation. Similarly, failure rates for juveniles released from training schools show a good deal of variability. A number of studies were reviewed by Gibbons (1968:517). He reports that whereas the majority of the males released from California facilities became reinvolved in delinquency, this figure differs considerably from institution to institution. In one investigation, for instance, it was found that violation rates ranged from a low of 36 per cent to a high of 60 per cent for boys released from different kinds of institutions. The low rate was for boys released from the "prison camps," which house younger, less serious delinquents. The higher figure, in comparison, was for boys discharged from an institution reserved for tougher, older, quite serious and experienced boys.

These figures should not be taken as definitive regarding the impact training schools have on delinquents. Most delinquents seem neither to improve nor to deteriorate substantially as a result of their incarceration experiences. Rather, juvenile institutions probably have a benign effect on their wards, so that neither success nor failure can be totally explained as a result of incarceration (Gibbons, 1970:261). In short, conventional correction appears to have little impact one way or the other on those subjected to it. This point is elaborated on below.

THE FAILURE OF TREATMENT

In the simplest sense, the output, or effectiveness, of a correctional program depends on two factors: input, or the type of individuals treated, and the correctional program itself. As far as the first factor is concerned, correctional officials are handicapped since they have only minimal control over the population they are to service. About the only recourse available to them is to classify offenders in some way so as to minimize custodial and administrative tasks and thereby increase resources for treatment programs. The differentiation of maximum- and minimum-security prisons and similar procedures are steps in this direction.

Still, the correctional staff is faced with a population of individuals most of whom do not desire treatment and do everything they can to frustrate treatment efforts. Even the best-intentioned administrator finds it nearly impossible to break through the defense system constructed by inmates to protect themselves from the impact of treatment efforts. Research (Sykes, 1958; Irwin and Cressey, 1964) has found that a strong inmate subculture can be located in prisons functioning to block any impact correctional officers may have on the inmate population. At the same time, this subculture provides a set of role patterns to which various inmates might subscribe that are quite different from the docility and subjugation prison administrators would prefer. Although there is some debate as to the origins and functions of this social system, the practical problem of breaking through it in order to deal effectively with individual inmates is yet to be resolved in institutional settings. Indeed, as Sykes (1958) suggests, the inmate culture is probably a product of institutionalization itself, so that institutionalization as a means of rehabilitation is self-defeating at the outset.

Custodial officials do have considerably greater control over the kinds of treatment they wish to initiate. With rare exceptions, however, little that takes place in conventional programs can be regarded as treatment. Neither prisons nor probation offer systematic therapy. And related activities seem to be only half-hearted attempts at rehabilitation. In many cases, these programs are initiated with something other than treatment as the primary goal. Correctional officials are much more concerned with the practical problem of custody than with the behavior of their inmates after release. The argument is often made that "you can't treat them if you can't keep them." Moreover, citizens become quite upset over prison breaks and demand some assurance that rehabilitation works before they will allow the conditions that might help to make it work. Releasing inmates into the community for work or recreational activities is not the kind of program most citizens would heartily favor.

As far as probation is concerned, the evidence indicates that most clients receive little if any counseling, which is understandable given the massive caseloads handled by probation officers. Where probation facilities even exist, studies have revealed that officers are inundated by paper work and other clerical duties or are caught up in the bureaucratic problems of keeping tabs on their clients' whereabouts.

Those who succeed on probation cannot, therefore, attribute their success to the services they received while on probation. Quite the contrary. Probation succeeds because of the kinds of people who get this disposition. Most of the individuals placed on probation are not committed to a life of crime, and most do not need any correctional assistance since they are likely to refrain from illegal activity in the future anyway. For these offenders, the best probation has to offer is social-service assistance and occasional counseling to help them manage living under conditions of spoiled identity. That is, they don't need to be "corrected." Instead, many could benefit from services designed to reintegrate them into the community, to help them find employment, re-establish personal relationships, live with an identity of "criminal," and the like.

Not only is rehabilitation lacking in prisons, but prisons are not geared to generating success for those who leave them. Nor is it likely that much can be done to alter this situation short of totally revamping the concept of imprisonment. This is not to say that prisons function to encourage further criminality. That is still an open question. I mean, rather, that prisons are not oriented to maximizing the conditions related to postrelease success.

Glaser (1964:504–13) found that rates of recidivism tend to vary inversely with postrelease employment. The more readily an ex-convict finds and retains employment upon release, the less likely he is to become reinvolved in crime. Yet, conventional penal facilities do not seem to have any positive effect on inmates' motivation to work much less pursue an occupation when released. Work training cannot, after all, make a dedicated employee out of an unwilling inmate.

The effect of prisons, as Wheeler (1969:120) concludes, also probably depends more on the kinds of individuals incarcerated than on the experience of incarceration or any treatment received. Professional thieves, for example, appear to be immune to the experience of imprisonment. These individuals tend to be committed to theft as a way of life. They relish the activity and see little reason to change. For them, imprisonment is but the price one pays to ply his trade—much like paying dues to a union. This is not, however, true of most other inmates, whether or not they succeed after release.

Glaser's (1964:511) argument is a potent one. He suggests that the principal factor in postrelease success is the individual's ability to resume a conventional social role and place in society, in spite of his history of imprisonment. Those persons who fail on parole, Glaser contends, do so because they never had the opportunity to experience a conventional life style in the first place. This is where contemporary correctional programs fail. The system is just not geared to inculcating the values, habits, and attitudes in inmates that would ensure their success upon release from prison. Hence, those who have never lived a conventional life are not likely to pick up the habit in prison.

The threat of imprisonment probably does deter some people from violating criminal laws; at least, it is an additional reason for those individuals who would probably not engage in criminality anyway to refrain from the practice. For many individuals convicted of wrongdoing, the experience of imprisonment seems to have a negligible impact; those who are prone to illegal activity are likely to continue in criminal ways in spite of imprisonment. On the other hand, it is likely that those who are not committed to crime would not have engaged in illegal activity again anyway. But for that proportion of the population that is deterred from further criminality because of imprisonment, it appears that this is not because the experience of incarceration serves to win them over to socially approved ways but because it instills an abhorrence of punishment in some of those who have experienced its impact. Corrections thus acts as a negative, not a positive, deterrent. But for many individuals the fear of punishment is simply not enough to deter the activity; for others, it may not even be necessary.

TREATMENT EXPERIMENTS

Considering the amount of attention devoted to rehabilitation, surprisingly few systematic experiments have been undertaken to increase the rehabilitative impact (deterrent effect) of criminal corrections. Even fewer studies have been designed to evaluate the few experiments that have been initiated. From time to time various programs are tried ranging in scope from the more extensive use of probation to full-fledged therapy ventures involving specially designed facilities and trained treatment workers.

Most of the more elaborate of these ventures have been tried on juveniles. Usually these experiments follow some form of psychotherapy or environmental (milieu therapy) type of program. Sometimes these two approaches are combined in institutions characterized by a residential home-like setting with a corresponding de-emphasis on custody and punitive activities. Usually inmates are subjected to group counseling, encounter-group therapy, and similar "treatment" efforts. All of these experiments basically seek to manipulate or control a set of factors thought to be important for treatment. The logic of these programs seems to be that if convicts do not improve in traditional prison surroundings, altering the environment may help. If leather shop or solitary confinement do little to deter criminals, they might be talked into reforming. Few of these experiments have met with marked success.

One of the most famous projects of this kind was the Highfields experiment carried out in New Jersey (McCorkle *et al.*, 1958). In this program 24 boys were placed in a small institution (the old Lindbergh mansion). A guardian-type staff consisting of a house "mother" and "father," various administrative and maintenance personnel, and a group of social workers replaced the usual custodial guards.

On the basis of the theory that delinquents are essentially normal but suffer from antisocial attitudes and negative images of themselves, inmates were given treatment consisting of group-counseling sessions and opportunities to work for money. In conjunction with this theory, research designed to evaluate the experiment sought to ascertain rates of recidivism, attitudinal changes, and alterations in the boys' personalities. These measures were compared with the findings of a similar investigation of a control group placed in Annandale reformatory (the regular training school).

First reports were encouraging. But several restudies of the experiment reveal that no marked or permanent changes in attitudes or personality took place in either the Highfields or the Annandale group (cf. Lerman, 1968). The recidivism rate for Highfields releasees was considerably lower than that exhibited by the Annandale group (37 per cent compared to 53 per cent), but over 18 per cent of the Highfields boys did not complete the treatment program. If this figure is added to the 37 per cent failure rate, it is clear that the Highfields project did not accomplish its goals.

A more recent program, similar in intent and design to the Highfields project, was initiated at Fricot Ranch in California (Jesness, 1965). In this experiment, officials sought to replace the 50-ward dorms, strict military discipline, rigid programs, and other prison-like features of the institution with smaller (20-ward) cottages and a less punitive program. This strategy it was hoped would effectively break down the inmate peer structure characterizing the institution. This, in turn, would allow treatment personnel greater access to and impact on the attitudes and personalities of the delinquents. Boys were randomly assigned to experimental and control groups, and comparisons were made on the postrelease success of these wards. Again, first reports were encouraging but after a three-year follow-up a violation rate of approximately 80 per cent was found for both experimental and control groups.

An experiment known as the Pico Project, though quite different from those mentioned above, sought the same goal. The attempt in this experiment was to maximize the amount of psychotherapy delivered to boys in an institution housing older, quite serious delinquents (Adams, 1962). Once again inmates were divided into control and experimental groups and then further categorized into types according to their potential as subjects for therapy. Both types of inmates were assigned to each of the control and experimental groups so that some of the youngsters typed as good candidates for treatment ("amenables") received no therapy whatsoever while some "non-amenables" were subjected to therapy even though they were judged to be lacking in the necessary attributes for treatment. In this way both the impact of treatment per se and its effects on different kinds of inmates could be assessed. If some treatment is better than none at all, one would expect the "treated non-amenables" to do better than either of the non-treated groups, although not so well as the "treated amenables."

This, however, did not prove to be the case. Both treated and non-treated amenables demonstrated the best postrelease performance, with the treated group doing slightly better. The treated non-amenables did worse than any group. Apparently, Adams suggests, the initial personality and attitudes of the boys had more to do with their postrelease behavior than did any treatment received. Indeed, treatment may be more detrimental than beneficial for some inmates.

The three studies mentioned above represent only a sample of the research available on various experiments of this kind. To date the majority of this research has been less than encouraging. To be sure, some programs show that costs can be reduced or that life can be made somewhat more bearable for inmates. But, over all, few differences are revealed in the postrelease behavior of the individuals dealt with in these programs. Ideally the goals of rehabilitation are desirable ones, but corrections have a long way to go before accomplishing them. Nor, given what is now known, is it certain that it would be desirable to do the kinds of things that may be necessary to achieve the ultimate in successful rehabilitation, no matter how laudable this may seem. People must ask themselves if they are willing to tolerate, in a free society, the kind of systematic thought reform, behavior altering and monitoring, and personality modification that might be prerequisite to rehabilitation. Unless they are willing to say yes with no qualifications to a full implementation of rehabilitative procedures, something less than total "success" in rehabilitating criminals will have to be accepted. In short, *the decision our society must ultimately make when considering the reality of rehabilitation is whether the individual is to be honored over the group or vice versa.*

PROSPECTS FOR REFORM

Numerous proposals have been advanced for reforming the machinery of corrections, ranging from improving dietary conditions to abolishing the institution entirely. Yet correctional programs remain pretty much as they were prior to World War II. Our society is not, apparently, quite ready to get out of the prison business altogether. Maybe it would be a mistake to do so, at least at present. Although imprisonment may have no specific deterrent effect on those exposed to it, it may be that the threat of imprisonment functions as a general deterrent. It is probably inevitable that some goats will have to be sacrificed to prisons periodically to keep the rest of us sheep in line.

Probably almost all of the reform proposals have been tried at one time or another. California has been especially progressive in this respect. So far, however, these programs have met with, at best, minor success.

Although the obstacles to reform are not impossible to overcome (cf. Morris, 1966), this writer has become increasingly pessimistic about the prospects for meaningful correctional reform in the near future. I see little to indicate that there will be any dramatic reductions in recidivism rates—which, supposedly, is what correctional reform is designed to accomplish, at least in part. This is not to say, however, that reform should not be tried on a wider scale. Efforts to make corrections more humane, efficient, economical, and equitable should continue, but not simply because of the potential fruit they might bear as far as "reforming" convicts is concerned. Change should be attempted because there is little reason not to do so.

Even though meaningful change probably would require a total revamping of the correctional institution, a number of effective reforms could be instituted in existing programs. The President's Commission on Law Enforcement and Administration of Justice (1967:166–85), for example, made several suggestions for improving correctional programs. Among other recommendations, the Commission advocated that more community-based treatment facilities be established to deal with offenders outside prison settings. Also, it was suggested that systematic criteria be established to supplant the rather arbitrary grounds presently used to decide length of sentence. For instance, some kind of formal classification system could be established to differentiate between individuals who should be placed on probation instead of in prison. Many incarcerated individuals, the Commission feels, should not be there. Imprisonment is costly to the state and often is socially damaging to the convicted criminal. Placing convicts who present little risk to the community on probation, the Commission argues, would save the state the expense of incarcerating them and spare the individuals the stigma, pain, disruption to family life, and the violation to self-image that results from prison confinement.

Moreover, the Commission recommends that convicts be classified in some way for treatment purposes. Some convicts, for example, could benefit from educational programs, while others might gain from job training. Still others may require only counseling for various purposes, and probably a few could profit from psychotherapy. At the same time, many inmates probably require no special services at all, while for others the expenditure of any effort to rehabilitate them is probably wasteful. Few systematic programs, however, exist at present to determine what kind of "correctional" handling is best for what kind of convict.

Efforts could also be made to improve conditions in the various institutions. The experience of European countries, notably Sweden, shows that the "de-prisonization" of correctional institutions by making the facilities more attractive and comfortable, less repressive and restrictive, may be beneficial and in any case is a just and humane objective. But, again, there is little reason to be optimistic about any results these reforms might bring. Why this is the case is fundamental.

In the first place, a prison is still a prison no matter what it may be called or how comfortable it is made. Imprisonment by its very nature negates the very possibility of rehabilitation. For the correctional system to do otherwise, therefore, the entire notion of incarceration would have to be abolished. Secondly, a number of writers have lamented that if the factors causing people to commit crimes were known, efforts to cure them would be more successful. But this argument is equivocal. It presumes something that may not be the case in fact.

It has already been contended that the whole notion of rehabilitation is grounded in an image of the criminal as a specific type-of-person. Rehabilitation is senseless without some notion of the criminal as sick—as in need of treatment (cf. Aubert and Messinger, 1958). This concept is not only dangerous but also of doubtful validity. It may very well be that persons convicted of crimes do not "need" treatment in any sense of that word. That is, their behavior may *not* be a result of some personal pathology amenable to cure. Many convicts may suffer from various difficulties—but there is reason to believe that for some individuals, at least, these difficulties arise from the experience of being corrected for criminal offenses. Nor has it yet been systematically demonstrated that the behavior corrections seek to change stems from these conditions. If this is the case, rehabilitation is useless. It may also be self-defeating.

That is to say, conceptualizing the criminal as sick is analogous to the practice of equating the pathological agents generating a disease with the observed symptoms of the diseased person. In a similar way, the sick character of the criminal is founded on the interpretation given to his behavior. The two may not be the same. In the past, the criminal was viewed as a bad person. He was known for what he was from the deeds he committed. Rehabilitation supposedly has dispensed with this mentality. In fact, it has only rephrased it. Today "sick behavior" is thought to be the product of sick people, and one knows that these people are sick because of their deeds. "Sick" has thus become but a new way of creating the social entity "criminal" and, as a result, the conceptual reality of crime. It is not the world that has changed but man's conception of it.

The end result is the same. The phenomenon created by the treatment process itself, whether that be punishment or therapy, is sustained. The character of crime has changed because the conception of the criminal has changed. But crime remains a feature of the world because members are able to find persons "in need of treatment," who fulfill their image of what criminal kinds of persons look like. Maybe, as it is argued below, the perpetuation of crime is just what the correctional system is actually, if not explicitly, designed to achieve anyway.

THE DRAMATIZATION OF EVIL AND ITS CONSEQUENCES

The social response to individuals considered to be criminal offenders, whatever the particular form of that response might be, is essentially a way in which members of society pass moral judgment, not only upon the breakers of law, but upon their own habits and ways of life as well. In this way, the values we cherish most are protected and reaffirmed. The criminal poses a threat to all we hold dear in life. Unless he is excluded, set apart from the group, the whole structure of our society, as we see it, would be placed in jeopardy (Durkheim, 1964; Reiwald, 1949; Erikson, 1964). Ultimately this is the meaning of criminal sanctions, and it is for this reason that some form of correctional activity is likely to be retained for some time to come. Either the criminal must be made over (rehabilitated) to be like ourselves, or he must be punished to show his differentness (inferiority) from ourselves. It is not merely that people do not wish to be identified with deviant kinds of persons. They cannot be identified with them and at the same time keep their own world from being shattered about them (Lofland, 1969). To tolerate the criminal is, after all, to allow a form of life that, by definition, departs from the moral consensus expressed by the act of excluding him from our midst. To allow the criminal to remain among us is to imply that he is one of us, like ourselves. And this then implies that we are not what we have assumed ourselves to be.

Why does society react to crime at all? Matza (1969) suggests, for example, that criminal persons may not actually be any of the things others define them as being. In fact, most of the sociological literature on criminal persons has demonstrated just this point. But from a common-sense point of view, to be a criminal is to be maladjusted or antisocial. It is to be immoral, wicked, weak-willed, psychopathic, or dangerous. In short, to be a criminal requires social intervention and correction (Matza, 1969:155). This intervention and correction often fail to produce the desired results. It is also possible that societal reaction has an entirely different and opposite consequence from the one sought.

In 1938, for example, Frank Tannenbaum (1938: 19–20) proposed that society responds to criminal activity by negatively defining and rejecting the offender. This response and rejection, he argued, can be described as a "dramatization of evil," which serves to identify to society the "evil" in its midst. Ostensibly individuals are deterred as a result of this reaction. However, Tannenbaum speculated, by responding to criminality in the way they do, society's members may actually encourage continuation of the very activity they sought to eradicate in the process. Paradoxically, Tannenbaum suggested, the harder society tries to eliminate it, the more the evil seems to grow. A number of explanations have been offered as to why this is the case. Two of these are discussed here.

Tannenbaum's rather provocative thesis was ignored by sociologists for some time. Even now little research is available to evaluate the theory. Does societal reaction actually operate as Tannenbaum says it does? If so, under what conditions and to what extent? Is it a universal result or specific to certain criminal types? Answers to these and related questions are hard to find. The thesis does, however, deserve closer scrutiny.

Initial acts of criminality could possibly be explained by a variety of factors including motivation, ignorance, or expediency (Becker, 1963:26). Some people break the law once in their lives and never again. Others commit numerous violations over an extended period of time, sometimes becoming totally immersed in a criminalistic subculture pursuing crime as a way of life. While similar, these two orders of phenomena are by no means identical and cannot be explained in the same way. Chapter 3 dealt largely with theories attempting to explain the genesis of specific acts of illegality. Our concern here is with several ideas that focus on systematic criminality, or the acquisition of a criminal role over an extended period of time.

Becker's (1963:30) arguments are pertinent. He suggested that one essential ingredient is the development of motives and interests oriented to illegal as opposed to legal activity. The question is: Under what conditions is one likely to develop these motives and interests? According to Becker, criminalistic (deviant) motives and interests are socially acquired, as are all other motives and interests.

By applying this idea to Tannenbaum's thesis, it becomes clear that one of the crucial steps in acquiring criminalistic orientations (and as a consequence one of the crucial steps in building a stable criminal career) is the experience of being caught and publicly labeled a criminal. In short, becoming a member of a criminal subculture may depend more on the actions and responses of others toward the offender than on any personal attributes he might possess (Becker, 1963:31). Under what conditions could societal response have this effect?

One possibility is found in Lemert's (1951:76) observation regarding what he calls "secondary deviation." Lemert defines this concept as follows:

> When a person begins to employ his deviant behavior or a role based upon it as a means of defense, attack, or adjustment to the overt and covert problems created by the consequent societal reaction to him, his deviation is secondary.

In this sense, criminal corrections could act as a causative factor generating continued criminality. This is not to imply that societal reaction in and of itself fosters crime as an adaptive mode. Rather, it is *how* society responds to deviance that generates the adoption of a pattern of continued criminal conduct. This is crucial both for an understanding of criminal offending as well as for the administration of criminal corrections.

What happens to someone who is socially defined as a criminal? In the most general sense, two things typically occur. First, the offender becomes identified, both to himself and publicly, as a different kind of person than he was assumed to be. He becomes labeled a junkie, a rapist, a thief, a murderer. In short, he becomes "stigmatized" and thereby relegated to the status of a lower form of human being.

Second, in the course of defining the individual as a criminal type of person, a process of "social degradation" takes place in which the evil this person has come to represent is socially recorded in the opinions others hold of him. Thus, the person is "ritually destroyed." The result is a total transformation of his former social self. He becomes, literally, a new social object (Garfinkel, 1956). The criminalization process, beginning with police apprehension, through judicial processing, and on to correctional handling, is a series of symbolic events geared to this ritual destruction and status transformation.

Even if correctional activity has a neutral impact on the convict's identity and conception of self, he still faces difficulties once he is released. How many fathers would be happy to see their daughters dating a convicted rapist? What bank is likely to hire an embezzler? Could a child molester land a job as a primary-school teacher? After all, the saying "once a junkie, always a junkie" is just another way of stating that people who deviate once are likely to do so again. Moreover, once a person's actions are defined as deviant, that label is seldom limited to the specific action that called it forth. Becker (1963:33-34) suggests that the deviant or criminal definition is a "master status" that controls a person's relationships with others. Persons defined as deviant or criminal in one respect are frequently considered deviant in other respects as well. It is felt that rapists not only are likely to rape again but can also be expected to engage in other forms of deviance. People are rarely considered to be specifically bad. Rather, once they show themselves to be "that kind of person," their specific "badness" is generalized to their entire moral character. This has some rather important consequences.

Treating a person as generally rather than specifically deviant cuts him off from participation in conventional social groups. This, in turn, serves effectively to reduce the labeled individual's life chances by denying him the rights available to others. As a consequence, it is difficult for him to conform to the laws and norms of conventional society. This may make illegitimate activities, if not more accessible, at least more attractive to him (Becker, 1963:35).

For example, Schwartz and Skolnick (1964) found that persons convicted of assault were less likely to be considered for menial employment than were individuals with no criminal record. Thirty-six per cent of the individuals without a criminal conviction were offered jobs whereas only 4 per cent of those with a record were so considered. It was also found that persons accused but not convicted of assault were handicapped in employment possibilities; only 12 per cent of these individuals were offered jobs. Even acquitted applicants with a letter from the judge confirming their innocence were less likely to be considered for employment. Only 24 per cent of these individuals were given a positive response. Apparently even the suspicion of criminality is enough to cast doubt on a person's social worth.

These facts, however, do not suffice to explain secondary deviation, for the argument fails to consider why an individual would choose illegitimate activity no matter how limited his legitimate alternatives. In short, the restriction of opportunities is not of itself causally determinant. The factors underlying a person's decision to follow an illegal course of conduct rather than pursue legal activity, regardless of how limited the legal options might be, must still be identified.

Earlier it was suggested that being defined as a criminal encourages a negative self-conception. A good deal of attention has been directed by sociologists to the role self-images play in human behavior. G. H. Mead (1934), Cooley (1956), and others have argued that a person's role performance or behavior is in many respects a function of how he views himself (his self-concept). A person's self-concept, these theorists argue, is a product of how he feels others see him. His perception of how others view him is, in large part, based on how these others in fact respond or behave toward him. Finally, the way in which others behave toward the individual is based on the category to which he has been assigned—his social identity. Insofar as defining a person as a criminal involves societal rejection of that person, societal response to crime, it follows, is itself a way of generating a criminal or outlaw conception of self on the part of the rejected individual. If he had not already acquired this image of self while in the hands of correctional officials, continued societal rejection in the form of opportunity restriction guarantees that he will do so. Paradoxically, it is also a way of making sure that he lives up to the expectations society has of him, that he continues to behave as people all along assumed he would.

The process, of course, does not always work out as outlined above. The degradation ceremonies are not always successful. The prophecies are not always fulfilled. The outcast does not always allow society to make an outcast of him. Sometimes criminals do go straight, in spite of societies' efforts. The question we must ask, therefore, is why doesn't degradation always work? Why doesn't the evil always grow in our midst? At least two mediating or intervening factors are probably at work.

1. By definition, responding to a person as a criminal involves a process of rejection and correction, as we have seen. Rejection, however, varies in kind, intensity, strength, and duration depending on a number of factors. Research just beginning to accumulate on this issue suggests that the nature of the rejection is a function of (a) characteristics of the offender (his class, race, sex, status, etc.) and (b) characteristics of the offense committed. The Schwartz and Skolnick (1964) study mentioned earlier illustrates these points. Whereas the unskilled laborer accused of assault found life difficult, a study of medical doctors convicted of malpractice revealed that they actually gained economically; most reported an increase in business after the law suit. In part this is a result of the physician's standing in the community, citizens' views of the offense, and the sympathy of colleagues, who made an effort to refer patients to their beleaguered comrades. The obvious conclusion is that not all persons accused of crime suffer the same consequences.

2. Some factors may also be at work that effectively insulate the person from the negative impact of his identity. The "techniques of neutralization" discussed by Sykes and Matza (1957) as ways delinquent boys justify their activity are relevant here. Included in their rationalizations are verbalizations that deny responsibility for the act, condemn the condemners, or deny any injury resulting from their activity. Sykes and Matza see these techniques as causative factors in the sense that they allow the boys to continue to engage in delinquency. It is more likely, I contend, that they protect the boys from society's negative evaluation of their behavior. More generally, the ability to justify one's conduct in terms of some acceptable or higher principles probably does much to insulate the person from society's wrath, assuming, of course, that he even cares what others think of him in the first place. Also, the extent to which an offender can find support for his actions from others may have much to do in curbing the impact of societal response. Draft dodgers, antiwar demonstrators, political prisoners, and similar violators of the criminal law are just a few examples of individuals who fit this category.

In summary, the impact of criminal corrections is by no means uniform or universal. Nor is it clearly understood. Research is sparse, so that about all that can be offered at this point are hypotheses for investigation. An analysis by Thorsell and Klemke (1972:401–2) lists six possibilities. They suggest that the labeling process "is likely to terminate existing deviant behavior and to deter further deviation" under certain circumstances:

1. If the labeled person is a primary rather than a secondary deviant.
2. If the labeling is carried out in a confidential setting with the understanding that future deviance will result in public exposure.
3. If the labeling has been carried out by an in-group member or significant other.
4. The more easily the label is removable when the deviant behavior has ceased.
5. The more the labeling results in efforts to reintegrate the deviant into the community.
6. If the label is favorable rather than derogatory.

On the positive side, societal response does serve to identify what is objectionable both to others in society and to the person who offends social laws. Maybe this is why society responds to crime in the first place.

A distinction should be drawn between public and private dramatizations of evil. Dramatizing the evil of behavior to the individual involved (private dramatization) may serve to discourage his further involvement in this kind of activity. The public dramatization of evil could accomplish this purpose for the body politic. However, the public and private dramatizations of evil and their respective effects may be innately inconsistent with one another. The public dramatization of a person's evil may operate to deter others contemplating this kind of activity, while, at the same time, generating further offenses on the personal level. In order to dramatize evil publicly, a concrete social object needs to be found to symbolize the evil this object now represents. Evil is not something that can be identified in the abstract. It is locatable in the being of a single social object. Hence, to show society what is degradable, an individual needs to be degraded. This negates the possibility of any private dramatization of evil, which defeats the very purpose for which evil is dramatized in the first place.

CONCLUSION

The foregoing analysis covers only a few of the issues pertinent to the investigation of criminal corrections. A massive body of literature is available on the subject. What is clear from this analysis is that in spite of numerous studies, proposals, arguments, and immense allocations of both human and material resources, the stated objectives of criminal corrections have a long way to go before being realized.

Reiwald (1949:66) states that:

> When we observe all the measures and precautions which society takes against the criminal with its courts and prisons, its police and social workers, there seems to be no doubt that people most earnestly wish to prevent crime, to protect themselves against its effects and, above all, to keep the criminal at a distance.

But yet, "Is the contention exaggerated, or does it speak the simple truth, that man has contrived his institutions for the combat of crime so that he may in fact maintain it?" (Reiwald, 1949:173).

These two statements by the same author illustrate the paradox described in this chapter. While Reiwald's second observation refers to the fact that relatively little effort is expended in apprehending, prosecuting and punishing certain criminal classes so that, for some, crime is encouraged and perpetuated, we can give this observation a somewhat different interpretation. Undoubtedly criminal corrections does little to deter continued violations and, in some cases, operates to encourage illegal conduct. But this is still a superficial realization.

Criminal corrections also helps to create the very phenomenon it was created to eliminate by reinforcing a preformed image of social reality. It would make no sense at all to "correct" individuals for criminal conduct if we were unable to conceptualize criminal types of persons. The "actual" world is a reflection of the "possible" world, the world social actors are able to imagine in their minds. New images of the criminal, new definitions of his nature and characteristics, will produce changes in the experienced world as well as in the way members respond to the realities they perceive as experienced. The increasing use of rehabilitation is just one example of this ever recurring process.

I avoided saying that rehabilitation is somehow better or worse than a system oriented to punishment. It is undeniable that rehabilitation does raise a number of moral and ethical (besides pragmatic) issues that are far from being solved. For the would-be penal reformer, it is more imporant to realize that rehabilitation is not likely to produce results substantially different from those obtained by conventional practices. Rehabilitation is not a cure-all. The substitution of rehabilitation for punishment will not rid society of crime or criminals. They will only change in form. Corrections, to be sure, does not "cause" crime. Rather, crime necessitates (that is, it cannot be conceived without) some kind of correctional response. The abolition of corrections either foretells or reflects the demise of crime. The continuation of corrections, on the other hand, in whatever form it may take, ensures the continuation of crime. Society will surely see some need for corrections as long as crime exists. But *as long as crime is a function of societal members' perceptions of the world—that is, insofar as crime is an artifact of their view of the criminal as an individual "in need of punishment" or rehabilitation—crime will continue to exist.*

7

Understanding Crime Rates

IN CHAPTER 1 it was suggested that two general conceptions of crime are to be found in the literature of criminology. One view defines crime as an instance of *behavior* committed by some person, and places primary emphasis on delineating the characteristics of offenders and the causes of crime. The alternative perspective treats crime as a *definition* of behavior, a label imposed upon conduct. Adherents of this view have attempted to describe the process, procedures, and effects of criminal labeling. The view of crime taken by the analyst colors the topic for analysis. This applies as well to the study of criminal epidemiology, or crime rates.

Criminologists interested in epidemiology have studied crime rates both as phenomena for investigation in their own right and as data for testing theories and hypotheses relating to matters quite different. Most criminologists would agree that a thorough understanding of crime cannot be achieved without some attention to criminal statistics.

OFFICIAL RATES: VARIABLE MEANINGS

Periodic reports are disseminated by the mass media pertaining to the amount and distribution of crime. Usually these occasion great alarm because the reports imply that the amount of crime is both high and increasing dramatically yearly. Citizens are warned that they have a lot to fear from crime and are advised that immediate and massive action must be taken to correct the situation. The Omnibus Crime Bill passed during the Johnson Administration is just one example of the kind of reaction that the publication of crime rates can generate (cf. Harris, 1969). Yet, as the opening paragraph of this chapter suggests, there is more than one way to interpret crime rates. Moreover, the kind of knowledge one acquires about crime depends upon the different kinds of inquiry these interpretations lead one to undertake.

Few efforts have been made by criminologists to collect their own statistics on crime. Most discussions therefore have relied on the "official rates" published by a variety of agencies, most notably by the Federal Bureau of Investigation in its annual *Uniform Crime Reports*. These statistics are based on information obtained from more than 8,000 reporting agencies and deal with a wide spectrum of criminal offenses that are "known to the police." These offenses are divided into Part I and Part II crimes. Part I crimes are used to construct the so-called Crime Index, consisting of seven major felonies that are likely to be brought to police attention.* Both the absolute number of these crimes and the rates per 100,000 population are reported.

Rates are calculated in order to "norm" or standardize the absolute numbers for purposes of comparison. For example, suppose that City A, with a population numbering 100,000, reports that 100 robberies occurred in the past year. Compared to City B, which reported only 50 robberies, City A certainly had more crime. But if City B's population is 10,000 it actually had more robberies per person (or per some number of persons) than did City A. In effect, City B had a higher robbery rate. Table 4 shows the total number and rates of index crimes reported in 1971 for communities of various sizes. As this table indicates, large urban areas (SMSAs) had more crime than other cities and rural areas combined. They also had a higher rate of crime, even higher than the national rate as a whole.

* Part II statistics deal with arrests for non-index crimes, such as drunkenness.

TABLE 4

Total Crime Index, United States, 1971

Region	Number of Crimes	Rate per 100,000 Population
United States Total	5,995,211	2,906.7
Standard Metropolitan		
Statistical Areas	5,173,916	3,546.7
Other Cities	436,145	1,890.7
Rural Areas	385,150	1,032.3

SOURCE: Abstracted from the Federal Bureau of Investigation (1971: Table 1, p. 60).

What sense can we make from these figures? Quinney (1970: 111–23) suggests there are at least four different possibilities. The most common view rests on a behavioral conception which treats crime as an instance of conduct. By this definition, rates of crime are read as more or less accurate measures of the actual or "true" *amount of criminality* (number of illegal acts) taking place.

Alternatively, it has been argued that not all the crimes occurring in a population are reported or recorded by official agencies and that what is counted as crime depends on a variety of factors. If crime is defined as a label imposed upon behavior, then crime rates reflect the labeling activity of official agencies. In this respect, crime rates are a perfectly accurate measure of the *amount of social labeling* produced by a population and are not indicative of the number of crimes taking place.

One could, of course, be egalitarian about the matter and suggest that both factors are involved so that rates reflect a mixture of the incidence of criminal conduct and the labeling activity of officials.

Finally, a somewhat different argument holds that whatever the phenomenon counted in crime rates, the fact that crime is counted at all has significance. In this view, criminal statistics can be interpreted as "indicators of the socially recognized volume of crime." They are "production figures" measuring the amount of concern a society is able or willing to register over crime.

These conceptions raise different issues and have different analytic implications for criminology. No matter how one chooses to interpret crime rates (and it is, after all, a matter of choice), the concern of major importance to sociology is to explain them, to account for their volume, distribution, change, and variation. Depending on how criminal statistics are interpreted, both the nature of the explanation and the problems encountered in explaining the rates will vary. In what follows we will look at a number of explanations that adhere either to behavioral or to labeling views.

THE INCIDENCE OF CRIME

If rates are read as measures of the incidence of some form of behavior, it must be assumed that some actual volume of that activity exists and that the rate of "known" activity (those acts counted to determine a rate) more or less accurately reflects or measures the actual or "real" rate. Since not all illegal activity is detected, reported, or recorded, official rates represent only a sample of the actual number of crimes that one might assume to have occurred. The problem, however, is that there is no absolute way of determining just how accurate official rates are. One can know neither how many of the actual crimes are counted nor whether the proportions of this "real" rate recorded in official statistics are equal for all types of crime. Nor is it known if these proportions are uniform from one jurisdiction to another or for different periods of time. This allows for a good deal of variability in the absolute numbers of crimes that one might estimate from official data. For example, as Table 5 indicates, estimates of the number of drug addicts in New York City have ranged from a low of 110,000 to a high of 200,000.

The problem of estimating the true rate from the official rates poses several difficulties for both policy decisions and theoretical concerns. A difference of 90,000 cases does, after all, make considerable difference. One way to solve this problem is to compare one rate with another. For instance, if crimes known to the police are compared with data on citizens' reports of victimization, one could estimate the extent to which the official rates accurately measure the crimes experienced, but possibly not reported, by citizens. Although this tactic has a number of drawbacks (cf. Hood and Sparks, 1970:25–32) one can at least deter-

TABLE 5

Differential Estimates of Narcotics Use
in New York City, 1970

Source	Reported Users	Estimated Number of Users
Federal Bureau of Narcotics	30,000a	110,000
NYC Police Department	25,675	200,000
Deaths Due to Narcotics, NYC Health Dept.	794	160,000
NYC Narcotics Register	94,700	190,000
NACC assessment of drug use in general population	38,000b	135,000

SOURCE: Mary Koval, 1971:12.

a Based on trend 1966-68.
b Based on incidence data from a New York State Narcotic Addiction Control Commission survey.

mine the degree of error to be found in official rates in this manner. As Table 6 indicates, the extent of this error appears to be considerable.

Several things are apparent from this table. For one, many more crimes are experienced by citizens than show up in official statistics. In fact, less than half of all possible offenses are even recorded in official crime reports, although this percentage does vary considerably by type of crime. Only 11 per cent of the auto thefts are not reported to the police whereas forcible rape is not reported in almost 70 per cent of the cases.

There are a variety of reasons for the failure to report crimes even though the individuals were victimized and knew it. Primarily respondents felt that the police would either not want to be bothered or were unable to do anything anyway. This again varied by types of crime (The President's Commission on Law Enforcement and Administration of Justice, 1967:22). In any case, the conclusion that the "real" rate of crime is actually several times higher than that reported by the FBI is inescapable. This observation is further supported by a number of studies reporting data about individuals' involvement in illegal conduct.

One early study of this kind was based on a sample of 1,800 men and women residing in New York State (Wallerstein and Wyle, 1947). Respondents were asked to indicate their involve-

TABLE 6

Comparison of Survey and UCR Rates
(per 100,000 population)

Index Crimes	NORC Survey 1965-66a	UCR Rate for Individuals 1965b
Willful Homicide	3.0	5.1
Forcible rape	42.5	11.6
Robbery	94.0	62.4
Aggravated assault	218.3	106.6
Burglary	949.1	299.6
Larceny ($50 and over)	606.5	297.4
Motor-vehicle theft	206.2	226.0
Total violence	357.8	184.7
Total property	1,761.8	793.0

SOURCE: President's Commission on Law Enforcement and Administration of Justice, 1967:21.

a Figures based on a survey which asked a sample of citizens if they had been victims of a crime between 1965 and 1966.
b Based on the 1965 *Uniform Crime Reports*.

ment in 49 offenses ranging from malicious mischief to robbery and assault. In all, 64 per cent of the men surveyed reported committing at least one felony. Involvement in larceny was admitted by 89 per cent of the men and 83 per cent of the women. Over 75 per cent of both groups admitted to indecent exposure. Comparatively, approximately 40 per cent of the women and 60 per cent of the males indicated they had committed traffic offenses.

Most "self-report" studies have focused on juvenile involvement in crime. In one of the more influential of these investigations, Short and Nye (1958) compared samples of students from middle-sized Midwestern and Western towns with a group of training-school inmates. Like other investigations of this type (e.g., Reiss and Rhodes, 1961; Erikson and Empey, 1963), this study revealed that most juveniles engage in a number of illegal acts, some quite serious, and often more than once. Almost 90 per cent of the Midwest students and over 80 per cent of the Western group admitted to fist fighting. Well over half of both groups had committed petty theft. And almost one fourth had been involved in gang fights. Short and Nye point out, however, that although most juveniles engage in a variety of offenses, those who wind up in training schools tend to engage in more serious violations more frequently than do those not officially recognized as delinquents.

A similar study by Akers (1964) sought variations in admitted delinquency among students at different levels in the social-class structure. Interestingly, this study found that the incidence of delinquency was greater for upper-class respondents than for lower-class juveniles. This is particularily significant since lower-class youths are much more likely to be apprehended and prosecuted as delinquents. Seemingly this phenomenon represents a bias on the part of legal authorities. However, it should also be noted that lower-class juveniles, according to this study, more frequently engage in the kinds of delinquency that are likely to be brought to official attention. For example, whereas over 36 per cent of the upper-class youngsters compared to 30 per cent of those in the lower class admitted to driving a car without a license, almost twice as many lower-class respondents admitted to auto theft (probably joyriding).

What should be noted about these studies is that juvenile delinquency is much more widespread than official rates indicate and that this activity is common to most juveniles, regardless of economic or ethnic background. For most, the activity is infrequent and quite trivial in nature, however. The findings of these studies parallel the results of victimization surveys. Both indicate that if we have a lot to fear from crime (as official reporting agencies seem to suggest we do), the problem is much greater than that indicated by official rates.

This is not to say that citizens do, in fact, have a lot to fear from crime. The fear of crime is probably much greater than the reality warrants. Indeed, Roosevelt's statement that "The only thing we have to fear is fear itself" applies quite appropriately to the fear expressed by many citizens over crime. Even if the official rates doubled or tripled, it is simply not true that the bulk of the American population is being systematically assaulted, raped, murdered and robbed by some underclass of villains. This is not to say that crime is not widespread in America. Rather, the kind of crime people seem to fear the most (common street crimes, like mugging and assault) are among the least frequent

TABLE 7

Homicide Rates for Selected Countries
(per 100,000 population)

Country	Rate	Year Reported
Colombia	36.5	1962
Mexico	31.9	1960
South Africa	21.8	1960
United States	4.8	1962
Japan	1.5	1962
France	1.5	1962
Canada	1.4	1962
Federal Republic of Germany	1.2	1961
England/Wales	.7	1962
Ireland	.4	1962

SOURCE: President's Commission on Law Enforcement and Administration of Justice, 1967:30.

and tend to be restricted to specific social and ethnic groups. A number of investigations (cf. Wolfgang, 1958) show, for example, that if one receives serious injury due to assault it is likely that the culprit will be a member of one's family or a close personal friend. People probably have more to fear from friends and relatives in their own homes than they do from any mad rapist roaming the streets.

Homicide is an appropriate example because it is likely to be reported with relative accuracy. As demonstrated in Table 7, our homicide rate, while higher than we might like, is small compared to that of other countries. Even if the homicide rate for the United States were doubled or tripled, it is still not true that Americans are especially prone to murdering one another compared to the citizens of other nations. Moreover, whereas the risk of being killed by an assaultist is 1:20,000, the probability that one will die due to an auto accident is 1:4,000. Americans are killed five times more frequently on the highway than by murder. In fact, twice as many people die each year from falls than from murderers (The President's Commission on Law Enforcement and Administration of Justice, 1967:19).

Even a superficial analysis of crime rates reveals that if an American is to experience crime at all it will be some form of property crime. Property crimes comprise over 90 per cent of all index crimes, and serious index crimes make up but a small proportion of all crimes. In 1971, for example, the national homicide rate was 8.5 per 100,000 population while burglaries occurred 1,248.3 times per 100,000 population (Federal Bureau of Investigation, 1971:60).

Crime rates also show considerable variation geographically, so that the chance that any person will ever experience crime and if so what kind of crime differ greatly depending on where he happens to live. As the President's Commission on Law Enforcement and Administration of Justice (1967:28) reports, crime rates in general tend to be higher for cities than for other areas and they tend to increase as size of city increases. Fifty per cent of all crimes against the person and 30 per cent of all crimes against property occurred in 26 cities with 500,000 or more residents, even though these cities comprised only 18 per cent of the total population of the United States in 1965. "One of every three robberies and nearly one of every five rapes occurs in cities of more than 1 million. The average rate for every index crime except burglary . . . is at least twice as great . . . in these cities as in the suburbs or rural areas."

Cities are not uniform in their over-all rates or their rates for various types of crime. Robbery, for example, shows a good deal of variation, as is indicated in Table 8.

TABLE 8

Robbery Rates in 1965—Fourteen Largest Cities
in Order of Size
(per 100,000 population)

City	Rate	City	Rate
New York	114	Cleveland	213
Chicago	421	Washington	359
Los Angeles	293	St. Louis	327
Philadelphia	140	Milwaukee	28
Detroit	335	San Francisco	278
Baltimore	229	Boston	168
Houston	135	Dallas	79

SOURCE: President's Commission on Law Enforcement and Administration of Justice, 1967:29.

TABLE 9

Victimization by Race
(per 100,000 population)

Offenses	White	Nonwhite
Total	1,860	2,592
Forcible rape	22	82
Robbery	58	204
Aggravated assault	186	347
Burglary	822	1,306
Larceny ($50 and over)	608	367
Motor-vehicle theft	164	286

SOURCE: President's Commission on Law Enforcement and Administration of Justice, 1967:39.

Even though New York City has a considerably larger population, its rate of robbery is only slightly more than half that of Cleveland. On the other hand, New York, Chicago, and Los Angeles are about equal in population but show considerable differences in their rates of robbery.

Not only do rates differ between rural and urban areas and between cities of comparable size, but even within cities. Again, in general, for most cities the rates of crime are higher in the central city and decrease as one progresses toward the suburbs. It is also a well-known fact that crime rates of almost all kinds (particularly those recorded in official reports) are characteristically highest in the most run-down, socially disadvantaged areas of the city. If crime is an urban problem, it is even more an urban slum problem. A number of studies show that residents of slum areas exhibit the most fear or concern over crime (especially crimes involving personal injury) and they are more likely to be victimized by crime. This is particularly true (with rare exceptions) for minority groups and poor citizens (Table 9). The victimization survey conducted for the President's Commission on Law Enforcement and Administration of Justice (1967:38–39) found that, with the exception of grand larceny, poorer citizens were much more likely to be the victims of serious crimes. This holds as well for racial groups. Nonwhites are much more frequently burglarized and the victims of serious personal crimes than are whites.

The question to be answered is: Why are rates of crime higher in cities than elsewhere, more frequent for poor persons as opposed to wealthy citizens, and higher for nonwhites than for whites? If it is assumed that rates reflect the occurrence of criminal acts, one is left with only one possible explanation: Urbanites, the poor, and nonwhites commit more crimes than other people. This is usually attributed to a number of factors. Essentially it is argued that there has to be something about urban living, being poor, or nonwhite that leads people to commit crimes. A variety of theories have been suggested purporting to locate this "something" about these groups that would account for their more frequent involvement in crime. We will have occasion to review several of these theories in a subsequent section of this chapter. For the present I want to analyze this general theoretical premise in light of the rates themselves.

THE PRODUCTION OF CRIME RATES

If criminal statistics are read as measuring the actual number of illegal acts, any or all of the hypotheses offered to explain the incidence of this conduct are plausible if not yet verified. But, as I have suggested, there is reason to question the accuracy of these statistics and also the interpretation commonly given to crime rates. It may *not* be the case that urbanites, poor people, or minority members are actually more criminalistic than everyone else. Indeed, it may *not* be the case that the amount of criminal behavior is increasing every year, that more criminal acts occur in the cities, and the like.

This is not to say that the rates are somehow in error. The problem of accuracy is not the issue here. It is, rather, to say that these statistics tell another story if read in a different way. If crime is defined as a label imposed upon behavior, the rates of crime reported by official agencies are perfectly accurate measures—of the amount of social labeling taking place in any society. They indicate the degree of concern a society has with crime. In short, they measure the productivity of official agencies.

In this light, variations in crime rates need not be explained as a result of differences in the criminality of groups. Our explanatory problem becomes a different kind of issue. The question to be answered remains essentially the same, but the kind of answer given differs. Behavioral interpretations of crime rates focus on explaining the differential distribution of behavior. A labeling approach, on the other hand, leads one to explain the likelihood that some persons' behavior will be labeled a crime while others' goes unquestioned. It is not why people act as they do but why some individuals are selected to be defined as having acted in particular ways while others are not that is of major issue (cf. Kitsuse and Cicourel, 1963).

At the most superficial level, crime rates and variations in these figures, both over time and from group to group, reflect a variety of factors other than the relative amount and variety of criminal offenses. For example, the proportion of police personnel to citizens seems to be an important factor. As the number of police increases, the probability that more crimes will be detected increases. Since more officials are looking for crime, more of it is likely to be found.

It could be that the relatively high urban crime rate compared to the rural rate can be accounted for by the fact that a higher ratio of police is characteristic of urban areas. Of course, rural areas could have fewer police because the residents of these areas perceive less crime, and consequently less need for police, than do the residents of urban areas.

Most people are familiar with the claim that crime rates show an annual increase substantially greater than the population growth would lead one to predict. Between 1960 and 1971, for example, the Federal Bureau of Investigation (1971:61) reported that total crime had increased by 158.1 per cent. Violent crime jumped by 146.2 per cent while property crime was up 160.1 per cent. Is it necessarily true that citizens actually became that much more criminalistic in ten years? Or could it be that changes in police recording policies are reflected in this increase? Some evidence suggests that this might in fact be the case. For example, in 1950 and again in 1966, the New York City Police Department was substantially reorganized. In both years, dramatic increases in recorded crime occurred. The burglary rate rose from less than 5,000 offenses to over 40,000. Similarly, when the chief of police in Chicago was replaced in 1961, crime jumped by 83 per cent (Hood and Sparks, 1970:37–38). Alterations in policy, crackdowns, and the like could all result in substantial changes in the official rates of crime without any alteration in the behavior of citizens having taken place. Sometimes these changes reflect priority and resource decisions, but more often they are a result of other pressures, usually political in character (cf. Hood and Sparks, 1970:39).

If police operating practices are influential as far as crime rates are concerned, then variations in these rates are to some extent a result of the differences in law-enforcement practices and the organizational factors that affect police departments. As we saw in Chapter 4, police arrest behavior is influenced by departmental organization. Professional-type police departments more often treat crime in an official manner, arresting higher proportions of petty offenders than departments exhibiting a nonprofessional orientation. This in itself could lead to higher crime rates in areas controlled by professional departments, although it is doubtful that it has any substantial effect as far as index crimes are concerned. But also, professional police are geared to the bureaucratic practices of record-keeping. Hence, they are more likely to record officially crimes that nonprofessional departments would ignore. Or it may simply be that professional departments keep more accurate records. If this is the case, as police professionalism becomes more widespread one can expect that rates of crime will increase accordingly. A similar result is likely to occur as police departments become more technically efficient.

A similar argument can apply to differences in rates for various ethnic and racial groups. Since the police do hold prejudice toward various groups, the behavior of individuals associated with these groups is more often called into question by the police and other authorities. What would pass for youthful cavorting among certain categories of juveniles is sometimes interpreted as blatant delinquency in others. Insofar as the police have different expectations and opinions of various social groups, the rates of crime recorded for these categories of people could differ greatly independent of any differences in behavioral patterns characteristic of the groups.

Alternatively, what citizens define as crime and what they report as crime to the police could have substantial effects on crime rates. As we have seen, relatively few crimes are observed directly by the police. And many "crimes" go unreported by citizens, so that what can be counted as a crime depends to an unknown extent on the perceptions and behavior of societal members. As far as it can be decided, there is no consistency in the proportions of reported versus experienced (perceived) crime. According to Hood and Sparks (1970:41), several factors seem to be in operation.

> Presumably, the two most important factors likely to lead to reporting are first a belief that the offense is sufficiently serious for some official action to be taken to recover property or deal with the offender and, secondly, a feeling that reporting will be a useful thing to do—either in leading to the apprehension of the culprit or to the development of better preventive measures. In other words, changes in public perception and evaluation of deviant activity, changes in the extent to which they feel the need for "outside assistance" in dealing with the deviant, and changes in the level of confidence in the police can all have a marked effect on the proportion of crimes reported.

In turn, these factors could reflect a number of other conditions. At the simplest level, an increase in insurance sales compensating people for loss due to theft could prompt them to report crimes they would otherwise brood over but take no action against. More significantly, fundamental changes in the social organization of modern society could lead to a higher incidence of reporting behavior and to changes in perceptions of what kind of behavior should be brought to official attention. Hood and Sparks (1970:43) observe:

> Increases in education, affluence, and civil rights for minority groups, the break-up of traditional slum life and increasing opportunities for social mobility as well as the influence of mass communications are all factors which might affect the reporting of crime. This is part of what Biderman means when he claims that "year-to-year increases in crime rates may be more indicative of social progress than social decay."

Ghetto residents may, for example, be gaining confidence that if a crime is reported action will be taken on their behalf. Or, as the absolute level of affluence and expertise increases in ghetto areas, the "What's the use?" attitude could be dissipating, increasing the likelihood that criminality that went unreported before is now being reported. But this has yet to be demonstrated empirically.

What should be apparent from the preceding discussion is that there is much more to understanding crime rates than one might assume at first. Considerable confusion still exists over how rates are to be interpreted. Possibly several alternative interpretations are appropriate depending on the context. But besides the controversy over what crime rates *do* measure, disagreement still can be found over what they *should* measure.

For instance, official rates are characteristically based on the number of reported crimes per 100,000 population. There is disagreement as to whether or not this is the best measure regardless of how accurate or inaccurate it might be. Some people have proposed that rates should be calculated on an age-relative population, like fertility rates, as opposed to using the total population as a base. It is also debatable whether rates should reflect the number of crimes committed, the number of persons committing crimes, or some combination of the two. It makes a good deal of difference if one person commits fifty crimes, or fifty people commit the same crime once each, or fifty people commit fifty different crimes.

At best, crime rates as they are presently constructed mean whatever they are interpreted to mean. Criminologists are still unable to say with any assurance or accuracy how many people in a population committed how many crimes (or acts definable as violations of law) how many times over any period of time. The fact that such judgments are made routinely represents a policy judgment that is more than inconsequential. This is especially apparent when the matter of explanation is addressed.

THEORIES OF CRIME RATES

In Chapter 3 we discussed theories of criminal etiology, regarding the causes of individual misconduct. Theories of behavior and of rates of behavior are related but are not interchangeable. Hence, theories of crime rates warrant separate discussion. Assume, for example, that it was known that some kind of mental pathology is responsible for causing people to commit rape. Now, suppose that City A has a higher official rate of rape than City B. In order to use the mental-pathology theory to explain this difference in rates, one would have to argue that more of the residents of City A suffer from this condition. This, however, does not suffice; one still has to explain why a higher incidence of mental pathology exists in City A than in City B. This requires that one construct a theory explaining the *epidemiology* rather than the *etiology* of rape.

Many different kinds of illegality take place, but much of this activity goes unrecorded in crime rates, for a number of reasons. Some forms of illegal conduct are rarely brought to the attention of legal authorities either because they are difficult to detect or because they are usually handled in an informal manner. Embezzlement and various kinds of employee theft, for example, are probably underrecorded in crime rates because companies often prefer simply to discharge the employee rather than bring formal charges against him or report the matter to the police.

In any case, official criminal statistics tend to be slanted toward certain forms of criminality, especially "garden variety" street crimes like mugging, assault, and burglary. Since criminologists largely rely on official statistics as their chief source of data, they have been severely hampered as they attempt to draw theoretical conclusions from these figures. That is, since official statistics on crime selectively emphasize certain types of illegal behavior, theorists trying to explain the rates and distribution of crime are highly restricted (to the extent that they rely on official statistics) in explanatory scope. Quite possibly a systematic bias would be found in contemporary explanations of crime rates if these theories were to be applied to a wider range of illegal activity. If, for example, consumer fraud and embezzlement were as systematically reported and recorded as are robbery, auto theft, and homicide, it is conceivable that theories of criminality would be quite different from those available at present.

This is not to imply that efforts to explain the amount and distribution of crime are unwarranted. Assuming (in the one case) that official rates more or less accurately reflect the relative occurrence of certain kinds of activity, it is not illegitimate to theorize as to why some groups seem to be more frequently engaged in this kind of behavior than others. The point is that theories that are closely tied to official data should be read with a good deal of caution.

For instance, official statistics indicate that the burglary rate is several times higher for nonwhites than for whites (both as victims and as perpetrators). Why these statistics look this way is indeed an important question to ask. Possibly nonwhites do, in fact, more frequently engage in a mode of conduct called burglary than do whites. Whites, of course, could be engaged in other kinds of criminality (like tax fraud) which are not systematically recorded in official statistics.

The problem is that the numbers that any theory seeks to explain do not tell us which of these possibilities is the case. What the rates mean, therefore, is something imposed upon them by the theorist. Hence, depending on how they are interpreted, different answers given to the same question may be equally valid. Theories do not provide pictures of "the truth." They merely reveal alternatively possible truths—several varieties of which are discussed below.

Social Disorganization   One of the first efforts to account for ecological variations in criminality within American cities is found in the writings of Clifford Shaw and Henry McKay (1929, 1942). Employing data taken from official records on the numbers of individuals referred to juvenile court, they found systematic variations in the rates of official delinquency for different geographical areas in Chicago and other cities. Although the patterns were not identical, Shaw and McKay established that the highest rates of crime can generally be found in slum neighborhoods located near city centers and that these rates decrease with increasing distance from the center. Subsequent research has found similar patterns in a number of localities.

The patterns found by Shaw and McKay remained fairly constant in spite of population changes over time. Areas in Chicago with high crime rates in 1900 also had the highest rates thirty years later. Since the ethnic composition of the areas had changed, and since the relative rates of crime for various ethnic groups also increased or decreased depending on their residence in these areas, Shaw and McKay concluded that ethnic composition alone was not sufficient to explain the variations in rates observed. Rather, something about the geographical areas themselves—areas which they called "delinquency areas"—must, they thought, be responsible for these high rates.

A number of variables were tested to see if differential crime rates correlated with various ecological features peculiar to the communities having high rates of crime. It was found that the highest rates closely correlated with factors that Shaw and McKay considered to be indicative of an underlying state of *social disorganization*. The most significant of these factors included high rates of substandard housing, mental disorder, population change, disease, poverty, and the like. In short, crime and human wretchedness seem to go hand in hand.

Detailed life histories of delinquents were also accumulated to trace the pattern and process of involvement in criminality (e.g., Shaw, McKay, and McDonald, 1938). On the basis of this evidence, it was argued that high patterns of delinquency occur in these areas because the areas themselves lack stability, cohesion, and, hence, social control. Criminality becomes a more or less traditional aspect of social life in these communities, and this tradition is passed on to subsequent generations primarily by means of play groups and gangs.

While a number of criticisms have been levied against this argument (cf. Rosen and Turner, 1967), research has persistently reaffirmed Shaw and McKay's findings, if not their conclusions (cf. Lander, 1954; Polk, 1957; Quinney, 1964). All these studies indicate that the organizational status of a community may, in fact, be related to the incidence of criminality exhibited by its members.

But why and how organizational factors operate so as to cause different patterns of criminality requires explanation. Social disorganization theory may have some value in explaining variations in rates, but only if it can also be used to explain the incidence of crime as such. It is one thing to say that differences in crime rates are a function of differences in the degree of social organization of various groups. It is quite a different task to show how organizational factors operate to cause the conduct supposedly reflected in these rates. Areas marked by social disorganization may exhibit a tradition of crime. The question however remains: How did this tradition arise in the first place? Presumably it stems from the disorganized character of the community. But it could just as well be the case that a criminal tradition operates to generate, or at least contribute to, the degree of organization found in any community. Ecological research has so far only been suggestive in this regard. A second theoretical school carries this line of thought a step further.

Anomie The term "anomie" has been used in a number of ways by sociologists (cf. Clinard, 1964). The man responsible for introducing this concept to sociology, Emile Durkheim (1947), employed the word in different ways himself. It is generally agreed, however, that relative "normlessness" and "social deregulation" come closest to the meaning intended by Durkheim. In any case, it was a state of anomie that Durkheim (1951, 1964) felt was responsible for the genesis of certain kinds of social pathology, such as suicide, and for dramatic changes in the rate of crime.

In contrast to the prevalent thought of his day (and current thought as well), Durkheim (1964:64–75) proposed a rather paradoxical argument. Even though criminal behavior is surely pathological in nature and is so treated by societal members, it is, he asserted, a normal condition of human group life. So long as the amount or rate of crime common to any society remains fairly stable, one can be assured that the society is in a state of health. It is only when dramatic changes in the rate of crime occur (either increases or decreases) that one should begin to worry. It is not the rate of crime, therefore, that has to be explained. Rather, it is changes (or differences) in this rate that are of significant sociological interest.

Durkheim offered an elaborate explanation to support his thesis. For one, he suggested that crime is normal because it is found in all societies of all types and for all periods of history. Its form may change, but "everywhere and always, there have been men who have behaved in such a way as to draw upon themselves penal repression" (Durkheim, 1964:66).

Crime is normal for another reason also:

> . . . because a society exempt from it would be utterly impossible. Crime . . . consists of an act that offends very strong collective sentiments. In a society in which criminal acts are no longer committed, the sentiments they offend would have to be found without exception in all individual consciousnesses, and they must be found to exist with the same degree as sentiments contrary to them [Durkheim, 1964:67].

Because, as Durkheim asserted, people differ in their values, goals, aspirations, and the like, it is simply impossible for all people to share sentiments to the same degree. But even if it were possible, "crime would not thereby disappear; it would only change its form, for the very cause which would dry up the source of criminality would immediately open up new ones." This is because a society cannot exist free of crime. Since it is both normal and universal, crime must be necessary or functional for society. Durkheim (1964:70) argued that crime "is bound up with the fundamental conditions of all social life." In this respect, crime is useful; it serves some necessity for the normal operation (evolution) of human society.

According to Durkheim, crime is useful for two reasons. One, insofar as rules, norms, and laws are essential to social life, crime is functional because its occurrence and the subsequent reaction to it reminds us of what these rules are. It reaffirms the moral values of the group and, hence, helps to promote social stability. Conversely, crime is also essential for social change. No society can remain stagnant and expect to endure. Change is both inevitable and necessary for society. The existence of crime, Durkheim suggested (1964:71), "implies not only that the way remains open to necessary changes but that in certain cases it directly prepares these changes."

Society responds to crime by punishing the offender. But, Durkheim cautions, society should not seek to eliminate it by responding too strongly. To do so would mark the eventual decay and death of society. It is not crime that poses a danger to society. Indeed, it is just the opposite. If a "normal" rate of crime is indicative of normality or a healthy social condition, abnormality in crime rates betrays some pathology in society.

A number of factors may precipitate changes in the rate of crime, but two conditions are primarily responsible. Society has either become overly repressive, thereby stultifying innovation and change while abolishing crime, or society has become anomic. The rules that control human behavior have lost their force. Society is in chaos. Crime becomes rampant. The two causes have different effects, but the implication is the same. Society itself is in danger of disintegration. More remains to be said about this idea. We will return to it in the concluding section of this chapter.

In spite of its profundity, this theory is only indirectly applicable to the phenomenon of crime rates. Durkheim provides some clues as to why crime would be present in some amount, but falls short of specifying what the rate would be for any given group or why rates differ from one area to another.* Several reformulations of Durkheim's thesis do attempt to answer these questions more directly. The most important of these revisions is Robert Merton's popular theory of social structure and anomie.

Merton (1956:131) sought to explain "why it is that the frequency of deviant behavior varies within different social structures and how it happens that the deviations have different shapes and patterns in different social structures." Like Durkheim, Merton located the causes of crime (deviance) in the basic nature of human society. However, he expanded this idea considerably by suggesting that "social structures exert a definite pressure upon certain persons in the society to engage in nonconforming rather than conforming conduct" (p. 132). Criminality and other forms of deviation are, therefore, adaptations to abnormal social conditions, not the products of abnormal personalities. As these pathological social conditions exert differential pressures upon various groups, and as the modes of adaptation available to counter these pressures vary from group to group, not only the rates but also the types of deviation found in these groups will differ.

In any society, Merton suggests, certain wants or aspirations— in short, certain culturally prescribed goals—are universally sought by societal members. At the same time, certain means of achieving these goals are institutionalized and normatively enforced as the right and proper ways. Usually society is organized so that an equitable distribution of means is available to members. However, should some disjunction between goals and means set in, substantially reducing the chances of some groups to achieve the goals, a state of social pathology can be said to occur. The commitment people have to the goals or the means

* Some suggestions are provided by Durkheim (1951) in his analysis of suicide.

made available to achieve them tends to weaken. Society experiences a condition of anomie. This state, Merton argues, is chronic in modern Western society.

Under conditions of anomie, individuals are forced to adapt to an essentially abnormal situation. They can do so either by rejecting (—) or by accepting (+) the goals while at the same time rejecting or accepting the legitimate means. Or they may substitute (±) new goals or means for the old ones. Thus there are at least five logical possibilities, as is indicated in Table 10.

TABLE 10

A Typology of Modes of Individual Adaptation

Mode of Adaptation	Cultural Goals	Institutionalized Means
Conformity	+	+
Innovation	+	—
Ritualism	—	+
Retreatism	—	—
Rebellion	±	±

SOURCE: Merton, 1956:140.

It is not clear which of these modes of adaptation corresponds to which specific forms of deviation. Most observers agree that innovation fits most closely with specific forms of criminality, especially property offenses such as embezzlement, robbery, burglary, and the like. If this is true, this theory could have some explanatory power as far as differential rates of this behavior among various groups is concerned, such as the disadvantaged or those individuals who are excessively power-hungry, and the like. But it hardly explains the rates per se.

For instance, Merton suggests that American culture places a great emphasis on success goals, particularly material wealth. At the same time, certain groups (e.g., nonwhites, young people, the uneducated, etc.) are excluded from the ordinary means of achieving economic riches. Unless these individuals reject success goals (e.g., adopt a form of retreatism or ritualism), they are either forced to remain forever frustrated or to seek new means (e.g., innovation) to achieve wealth. Apparently large segments of the disadvantaged groups in our society have selected just this route, at least if one chooses to read criminal statistics at face value.

Merton's theory has been both praised and criticized in the literature on a number of grounds. One shortcoming of the thesis was pointed out by Richard Cloward (1959), who suggested that the unequal distribution of legitimate means was not enough to explain differential rates of criminality. For some people, crime is simply not a viable alternative. They could not break the law even if they wanted to. The theory, therefore, has to be expanded to account for the relative distribution of both legitimate and illegitimate opportunity structures. Only then will it constitute a viable contribution to our understanding of the variations to be found in rates of crime.

Culture Conflict The schools of thought mentioned so far share one thing in common: They conceive of society as basically stable with general value consensus among members. Periodic disruptions may take place, but the fundamental structure of society remains sound. Crime is both a result and an indicator of some kind of social pathology, some malady of the social system. Crime may be functional for society, but the notion that the existence of crime (or, in Durkheim's sense, peculiarities in its rate of occurrence) suggests that something is wrong with society is clearly implied in these theories. The implication is that society must be reorganized in some way so as to decrease the amount of crime among certain groups or in society as a whole.

As we saw in our discussion of law, an alternative view is possible. Some writers have suggested that social systems exist in a constant state of conflict and change. It is not that all members are oriented to the same goals and turn to crime only when access to these goals is blocked. It is, rather, that subgroups within society are oriented to fundamentally different and largely incompatible goals. Groups whose goals and corresponding life-styles depart too much from those considered appropriate by the dominant group find themselves in conflict with the criminal code, which, as we saw, is a device created and used by the dominant groups to confirm and sustain their power. Different rates of criminal conduct are, thus, a result of the degree of intragroup pluralism of a society and the degree to which subgroups of that society are in moral conflict.

This general premise, which is more thoroughly developed in the work of Sellin (1938), Turk (1966), and Vold (1958), has had a decisive influence on criminology. Most of the literature in this tradition has postulated cultural conflict as a cause of criminal conduct. Usually differentials in official rates of crime have been taken as indicative of differentials in the actual amounts of criminal behavior for various groups. Most writers have sought to show that in groups with higher rates of crime, behavior labeled criminal by the society may frequently conform to subgroup norms, even though it violates the criminal code. Sellin (1938), for example, attempted to show that different rates of crime for various immigrant groups were directly related to the clash between traditional old-world conduct norms and the new-world situation. Whereas making wine at home, for instance, was a respected and proper activity in the old country for some immigrants, it was considered illegal in the new setting. People who were unwilling to give up the old ways were, thus, frequently the subject of legal sanction.

Moreover, for many groups, activities that were once considered appropriate were found to be out of place in the new surroundings. As a result, efforts to mediate between often conflicting traditions among individuals led to committing acts deemed illegal by both groups.

A more recent version of this idea, forming a general theory of crime rates, has been offered by Richard Quinney (1970a:15–23, Chapter 7). Rather than address rates of behavior, as the cultural conflict theory does, Quinney explains the probability that any given act will be defined as criminal.

Quinney suggests that criminal statistics constitute measures of the amount of criminal labeling taking place in a society. From this perspective, crime rates are an indicator of the kinds of behavior that the people who have the power to apply the criminal label seek to repress. The behavior of groups labeled criminal is conduct that conflicts with the goals, values, interests, or whatever of the power-holders. Even though there may be a general consensus in society that certain kinds of activity (e.g. murder, rape, robbery, etc.) should not go unpunished or present some threat to the group (cf. Gusfield, 1967), the conduct with a high probability of being defined as criminal is activity that conflicts with the interests of the power-holders. Insofar as these acts are differentially distributed throughout the population, the rates of crime exhibited by various groups will differ in accordance with this distribution. This theory explains the differences in crime rates within a society. Differences between societies can be explained as a result of the different degrees of intergroup conflict experienced by these societies. We can expect the rate of criminal defining to increase or decrease, or to be higher or lower for one society compared to another, depending on the extent to which subgroups within a society are in conflict with one another.

Crime rates, in this view, do not reflect the amount of criminality in a society. Rather, they measure the degree to which groups in a society conflict with one another. An increase in the rate of crime does not, therefore, mean that citizens are becoming more criminal. It means that the power holders are becoming more repressive. These points require elaboration.

In our overview of etiology, we saw that a variety of theories are available purporting to explain criminal conduct on the part of individuals. Of all these theories, only one, Sutherland's theory of differential association (Sutherland and Cressey, 1966), was said to make any kind of explanatory sense. Now, if a person's "criminal" behavior can be explained in terms of his learning experiences, it follows that different group patterns of behavior can be explained in terms of the differential distribution of learning experiences. A homogeneous society is likely to have relatively few differences in learning experience. Hence, behavioral patterns will be basically similar. Conversely, in a heterogeneous or pluralistic society considerable differences are likely to exist in cultural environments. As a result, learning experiences will be diverse, and, consequently, such a society will exhibit a variety of behavioral patterns.

In a pluralistic society, wherein a variety of behavioral patterns can be found, consensus as to appropriate, desirable, or acceptable behavior is less prevalent than in a homogeneous society. In short, disagreement or conflict between groups over proper conduct is more probable, but, of course, not inevitable. It is also likely that these groups will exhibit differentials in power.

Given that the behavior most likely to be defined as criminal is that conduct which conflicts with the interests of groups that hold power, and given that behavior counted as crime (in the form of a rate) is equivalent to behavior the power-holders seek to repress, it follows that pluralistic societies with a good deal of intergroup conflict (such as an urban mass society like our own) will exhibit the highest rates of crime, Conversely, societies with low conflict, which usually (but not necessarily) corresponds with the degree of pluralism, will have the lowest rates of crime (cf. Gibbs, 1962). This is illustrated in Figure 3.

Degree of Subgroup Conflict	Degree of Pluralism[a]	
	Homogeneous	Heterogeneous
High	Moderate Crime Rate I	High II Crime Rate
Low	Low Crime Rate III	Moderate IV Crime Rate

[a] This refers to both the demographic composition of a society and the power differentials between subgroups.

FIGURE 3
Types of Social Organization and Expected Crime Rates

The rate of crime in cell I is likely to be somewhat higher than that found in cell IV but less than cell II and more than cell III would exhibit because of conflict differentials. Since no perfectly homogeneous society is ever likely to be found, there is always room for conflict between subgroups, in which case the degree of subgroup conflict is the more important explanatory dimension.

In conclusion, the notion of differential association goes a long way toward explaining individual conduct. The paired concept of "differential social organization" provides some understanding of the distribution of this behavior. Together they could offer a viable explanation of crime rates.

But differences in behavior between two groups are not sufficient to explain variations in their rates of crime. It is not simply because people behave differently that they have different amounts of official criminality but because someone chooses to treat the "different" behavior of some groups as criminal. It is, in short, only when one group views the behavior of another as undesirable, threatening, immoral, or wicked that a rate of crime is likely to be found for that group. If the defining group also has the power to enforce its evaluation, then that possibility can be made a reality. This is to say that behavioral differences are not the sole cause of differences in crime rates, or of their absolute size either. That is, differences in crime rates not only reflect behavioral differences, they also indicate the degree of conflict between groups that have differences in relative power. The key to crime rates is not, therefore, the degree of a society's organization. Rather, the notion of intergroup conflict is what opens the road to theoretical understanding.

VARIATIONS ON A THEME

Durkheim teaches that crime is both inevitable and necessary. Since, by Durkheim's own admission, one can never find a society free of crime, his explanation of crime's inevitability is untestable. It must remain an interesting and provocative speculation. This is not to say that Durkheim was necessarily wrong in his claims. He did, after all, provide some crucial insights that further criminology's understanding not only of crime but of society as well.

Durkheim considered crime as an act that offends strongly held collective sentiments (in contemporary usage, values). Since people are not identical, some people, he thought, are bound to behave in ways that offend others and activate efforts to repress this behavior. In this regard, Durkheim operated on a behavioral conception of crime. Yet, as we have argued, crime (or deviance in general) "is not a property *inherent* in certain forms of behavior, it is a property *conferred* upon these forms by the audiences which directly or indirectly witness them" (Erikson, 1964:11; emphasis in original).

Although Durkheim implied a recognition of this principle, he failed to pursue it. He asked why people deviate in different ways and with different frequencies. He did not ask why behavior is labeled at all, or why the property "criminal" is variously conferred on the behavior of different groups with differing rates of frequency. Given what is now known about crime rates, an answer to this question is crucial. One possibility is found in the writings of Kai Erikson (1964, 1966), who draws quite heavily on the Durkheimian tradition.

It is Erikson's thesis that social groups label behavior as deviant (or criminal) in order to draw the moral and behavioral "boundaries" of the group. If society did not do so, it would apparently begin to lose its "distinct structure" and "cultural integrity." Society would disintegrate as a viable system and cease to exist. Erikson (1964:15) puts it in this way:

> People who gather together into communities need to be able to describe and anticipate those areas of experience which lie outside the immediate compass of the group—the unseen dangers which in any culture and in any age seem to threaten its security. Traditional folklore depicting demons, devils, witches, and evil spirits may be one way to give form to these otherwise formless dangers, but the visible deviant is another kind of reminder. As a trespasser against the group norms, he represents those forces which lie outside the group's boundaries: he informs us, as it were, what evil looks like, what shapes the devil can assume. And in doing so, he shows us the difference between the inside of the group and the outside. It may well be that without this ongoing drama at the outer edges of group space, the community would have no inner sense of identity and cohesion, no sense of the contrasts which set it off as a special place in the larger world.

Why, then, should different segments of society exhibit different rates of crime? This question as follows should be translated: Why is the behavior of some segments of society more frequently assigned the label "criminal"? Erikson does not supply the answer. It is not, however, difficult to discern if one keeps the notions of power and conflict in mind.

The highest rates of crime take a distinct pattern. They constantly occur among the most disadvantaged, disenfranchised, powerless segments of society. It could, of course, be argued that this is so because these groups are actually more criminal. But this misses the point. It is not only that these individuals behave in offensive ways. It is that they are perceived by others in those terms. In the case of crime, the others happen to be those who have the power to make their judgments stick.

Society is not, nor has it probably ever been, a single unified community. It consists of groupings each of which is concerned that its own boundaries (cultural integrity) be preserved. In Erikson's terms, in order to retain this sense of group, of belonging, others not like themselves must be excluded from the group. Indeed, to have a "group" at all, some others must be seen as outsiders. They must be defined as nonmembers if only to confirm the in-group's own sense of solidarity. Human beings, apparently, cannot survive as amorphous beings. The inevitable by-product of this is that those individuals cast outside the group are perceived by the members comprising the group as not like themselves and, conversely, the in-group members come to see themselves as not like "those other people."

The middle-class, suburban accountant gains a sense of moral worth as well as belonging by contrasting his behavior with that of some other person he defines as being not like himself. And if the other's activity can be cast in a negative light, so much the better, for it shows how much more laudable is his own. By defining the other's conduct as threatening, harmful, or disruptive—better still, by giving it an identity as criminal conduct, one adds further validation to one's own righteous purity (cf. Lofland, 1969).

Even though the members of one's own group may behave in ways similar to the outcasts, this conduct is, after all, only occasional and it is understandable in light of extenuating circumstances. When others not like oneself do it, however, it is expected and, thus, not excusable. "Just look at the way they live!" Of course, if something is expected beforehand, it is likely to be found when searched out. At least considerable energy is expended to find it.

This brings us back to a point mentioned earlier. Official crime rates are highly selective in the kinds of criminality they record. It is revealing that the kinds of behavior counted in official rates just happen to be peculiar to certain groups. The middle-class executive, for example, is not likely to commit burglary. He doesn't need to. But price fixing is within his realm of possibility. Laws restricting this kind of conduct exist—true. They are, however, loosely formulated and seldom enforced—not only because it is difficult to do so. The frequency of this conduct may actually be much higher than that of burglary or other forms of conduct typical of the powerless classes. But it is rarely noticed or counted. One can only wonder why. Indeed, one can only imagine what patterns would appear in crime rates were the powerless able to decide what is to be recorded. But then they would no longer be powerless.

8

Concluding Remarks: The Study of Criminology

MOST STUDENTS TAKING COURSES dealing with criminology probably do so in the expectation that they will learn all there is to know about criminal types of people. Many come with hopes of being offered explanations of and solutions to what they see as a pressing and important social problem. These hopes are frequently disappointed, for criminology has very little to offer by way of explanations and less still with regard to solutions. For other students, the study of criminology promises vicarious involvement in a world they would not think of entering themselves. Like disasters, accidents, and horror stories, criminology seems to hold a morbid fascination for these individuals. They too depart with a feeling of disappointment. The dry, systematic analyses characteristic of criminological writings simply cannot compete with the excitement of *Mod Squad,* the daily newspapers, or a James Bond film. Compared to fiction and the mass media, academic criminology seems dull indeed.

Both of these groups of students see crime only in terms of the criminal offender. When they think of crime they envision mass murderers, a rapist, a gangster or a drug-addict mugger. Many of their professors share a similar perspective.

This book devotes very few pages to the criminal. Hasn't

187

something been left out? Note the following statement by Thomas Szasz (1970:123).

> Suppose that a person wishes to study slavery. How would he go about doing so? First, he might study slaves. He would then find that such persons are generally brutish, poor, and uneducated, and he might conclude that slavery is their "natural" or appropriate social status.

Substitute the words *crime* and *criminals* for *slavery* and *slaves* and this statement would be a reasonably accurate summary of a criminology limited to studying the criminal. Indeed, it would be a description of what the bulk of criminology actually does look like. But, as Szasz (1970:124) continues,

> Another student, "biased" by contempt for the institution of slavery, might proceed differently. He would maintain that there can be no slave without a master holding him in bondage; and he would accordingly consider slavery a type of human *relationship* and more generally, a *social institution,* supported by custom, law, religion, and force. From this point of view, the study of masters is at least as relevant to the study of slavery as is the study of slaves. [Emphasis in original.]

This perspective is close to the one I have sought to emphasize in the preceding pages. I am not suggesting that criminals are similar to slaves or that crime is analogous to slavery. I am contending that crime must be viewed as a process, a set of "methods" (tactics, procedures, grounds, and rationalizations), for both creating and confirming an image of social reality. One cannot, that is, gain an adequate understanding of crime merely by studying criminals. But, some would argue, how can one ignore criminals when investigating crime? People, after all, *are* robbed, murdered, mugged, and raped. Somebody is responsible for these events. Since these things do take place, do we not have the right—in fact, the obligation—to study the people responsible? Whose side are you on, anyway?

This question has been answered in part within the pages of this book and was directly addressed by Howard Becker (1967) in his analysis of the labeling approach to deviance. A number of arguments could be offered on both sides. It is not, however, a matter of choosing sides. It is a question of constructing a viable and meaningful criminology; one that does more than simply provide descriptions of certain human types, one that reveals the underlying features of the social world rather than just encoding its perceived and obvious characteristics in the jargon of some science.

TOWARD A HUMANISTIC CRIMINOLOGY

In recent years criminology has undergone criticism on a number of fronts, particularly by members of the discipline itself. Most of these criticisms deal with technical matters such as the theoretical shortcomings of certain schools of thought or the limited scope of criminology's focus of inquiry. These objections can be readily overcome by increasing sophistication in research methodology and criminology's range of subject matter.

One criticism goes to the very heart of contemporary criminology by attacking its central philosophical premise. A number of writers, for instance, have argued that criminology has acted as a servant of the state. Criminologists, it is lamented, have allowed themselves to become lackeys of political repression. Acting as "consultants" to those who possess political power, criminologists have aided and abetted those who would negate the very rights that are the innate property of all human beings. By providing information to those who manage the existing social arrangements that precipitate social injustice, inequality, and repression, criminologists are, it is said, partially responsible for the present plight of humanity. This is so for two reasons. For one, it can be argued that criminology's emphasis on studying criminals provides a kind of scholarly credence for political authorities. This is especially true since criminologists tend to concentrate on the criminality of lower-class (powerless) groups. This has led them largely to ignore the crime characteristic of the more powerful upper classes. Second, it is argued, by concentrating on the criminality of lower-class members, criminologists have not only helped to legitimize the power-holders' evaluation of this group but also provided the rulers with knowledge for solidifying their power over the disadvantaged.

Few criminologists would seriously contest this contention. At least they would hold no quarrel with the idea that criminologists have accommodated state authorities by providing them with information on criminal types of persons. Even though concrete evidence to support this claim is lacking, most criminologists are well aware of what the discipline has been about for many years. Actually, it could be the case that academic criminologists are paid much less attention by political authorities than they would like to think. But the argument is serious enough to deserve contemplation.

A variety of explanations and suggestions on how to correct this state of affairs is offered in the literature. One argument lays the problem primarily at the doorstep of the concept of crime favored by most criminologists. In an insightful and compelling analysis, Herman and Julia Schwendinger (1970) suggest that most contemporary criminologists operate with a legal definition of crime. The nature of their subject matter is therefore determined by the agents of law, not by the criminologist. Having adopted this concept of crime, criminologists, the Schwendingers argue, mislead themselves into thinking they have displaced all bias in their pursuit of scientific understanding. In fact, they have become co-opted by the state while relinquishing the ethical and professional standards of their discipline. As the Schwendingers (1970:142) state: "The profession of ideological neutrality on their part was by no means a guarantee of this neutrality. Instead, it was one of the great myths which prevented principled scholars from being aware of the ideological character of their basic theoretical assumptions."

Criminology must, it is argued, change both its operative conceptions and its focus of inquiry. According to the Schwendingers, this requires that criminologists reconceptualize crime in moral, rather than legal, terms. Furthermore, they suggest that the central business of criminology is to act in defense of basic human rights. In order to do so:

> Criminologists must be able to identify those forms of individual behavior and social institutions which should be engaged in order to defend human rights. To defend human rights, criminologists must be able to sufficiently identify the violations of these rights—by whom and against whom; how and why [Schwendinger and Schwendinger, 1970:146].

While I am in basic agreement with the idea that criminologists have stood in a servile relationship to political authorities, I have elsewhere (Hartjen, 1972b) questioned the explanation offered by the Schwendingers and their proposal for reform. In that essay I sought to argue that a legal conception of crime does not compel criminologists to operate as consultants for political authority. In fact, criminologists have probably acted in this capacity because it pays well and because they share the correctional aims of the state. In short, it has yet to be shown that espousal of a definition of crime based on law predisposes one to practice repressive criminology. Quite the contrary. An approach to crime which stems from and thereby addresses the law and legal practices is a firm ground for developing a truly humanistic criminology. It is not the legal concept of crime that is to be disparaged but the use criminologists make of it.

What would a humanistic criminology be like? What would be its essential ingredients? Obviously, humanistic criminology must, at minimum, be oriented to protecting fundamental human rights. It should also be dedicated to helping people to secure these rights wherever and whenever they are violated. That is, a humanistic criminology is an active enterprise, involved with the world and disposed to ensuring that tyranny, repression, and oppression are fought on every front, no matter what form they take or by whom they are practiced. What role the individual criminologist should play in this effort is, of course, to be decided by him alone, depending on his talent, personality, and dedication. As practitioners of a scientific discipline, however, our task is clear. Before criminologists act in defense of humanity, they must first be able to identify the sources that threaten it. In this respect, the primary objective of criminology is to achieve criminologic understanding.

One way to do this is to adapt, with all its ramifications, a legal definition of crime. Not just any legal definition will do, however. If, for instance, one defines crime as *behavior* that violates criminal law, one is led to study those forms of conduct, as well as those persons engaged in them, which political authorities (the creators of law) seek to repress (control). Information obtained in this inquiry could then be used by political officials to carry out legal repression.

If, on the other hand, a definition of crime devoid of behavioral implications is truly adhered to, one that treats crime as itself a *definition* imposed on members by the agents of law, one is then led to investigate the masters as opposed to the slaves. As I have suggested, a definition of crime based on the notion of criminal labeling requires that the criminologist study the act of interpreting (labeling) behavior as criminal. To do so requires that one investigate those individuals or groups engaged in social labeling. Only thus can sufficient understanding be gained in order actively to protect against legal oppression.

Both crime and human rights are political phenomena. They are, in the end, a function of state authority. The study of crime that follows from the legalistic approach is the study of not only the operations of state authorities. It is also an inquiry that involves a questioning of the state. By truly adhering to the legalistic definition one is not automatically led to support of the state. Rather, one is automatically led to an evaluation of political authority—its practices and its grounds—which would necessitate holding that authority in question (Hartjen, 1972b:66).

According to Quinney (1971:ix), "Those who rule have the ability to define the rest of us as mad." By so doing the rulers strengthen their positions of dominance. Oppression by those in positions of political power is one instance of the violation of human rights. History is filled with examples. As free citizens, we not only have the right to be protected against those who would victimize us in criminal ways. We also have the right to be protected from legalized oppression by those who have been granted the responsibility of guarding our lives, property, and well-being. For this reason alone, the agents of the state are legitimate subjects for criminological scrutiny.

Violations by government officials, whether of codified law or some higher moral standard, are, like the garden variety of crimes typically studied by criminologists, obviously relevant to criminology. But the state can violate human rights in other ways as well. Even if legal authorities were to act as benevolent despots, refraining from using the full force of their power except within the rules of due process, the state authorities would still occupy a position central to human rights and, thus, remain within the realm of criminological inquiry. It is not political crime that I am speaking of here but the crime of politics. The state, that is, can play a passive role by failing to enforce laws deemed essential to securing, maintaining, or more equitably distributing

The Study of Criminology 193

human rights. The government's inactivity in enforcing civil rights legislation is just one example of this. Or the state could neglect to enact such laws in the first place. Or it could fail to act against individuals or institutions that actively or passively interfere with the rights of all. In any case, a criminology that neglects to keep a sharp eye on those who hold the power of political office (or those who work for them) cannot call itself humanistic.

ACQUIRING CRIMINOLOGIC UNDERSTANDING

Knowledge of the world is always and everywhere a product of the knower's own mind, an artifact of his theoretic creations. If, then, the world-as-known is a function of the act of knowing (theorizing), the reality investigated by scholars (in any field) is first and foremost located in the very theoretic creations designed to describe this world. By implication, this suggests that the criminologist's scope of inquiry is much broader than traditionally dictated, including within its bounds the theorist's own conceptual reality and the realities produced by others. This means that criminologists are to treat their own views, understandings, knowledge, and opinions as problematic, as something requiring investigation. Criminologic productions (i.e., theories, research reports, descriptions, analyses, etc.) are, thus, relevant resource materials for criminologic research (cf. Douglas, 1967:255–70). In other words, insofar as the "knowledge" produced by criminologists is reflective of a world seen (conceived) by them, and insofar as the world thus conceived is revealed (contained) in expressions of that knowledge, the verbalizations of that world are an important source of analytical material.

The content or composition of criminologic knowledge, however, is limited by what is known, by what is or has been studied. In this respect, the world-as-known is restricted to the lived experiences of its creators. One important means of gaining experience, of conceiving and thus constructing the world, is by scientific research. So far criminology's experience has been confined to investigations of individuals defined as criminals. The scope of criminologists' understanding (and, hence, of their world) has been severely circumscribed by the scholarly interests of criminology and the limited reality this interest has led criminologists to explore. As a humanistic criminology is one that is involved with the world, criminologists must become more immersed in their subject matter. This is to suggest that criminologists should extend their topics of inquiry to new realms of experience. Constructing new conceptions of the field's subject matter is one step in achieving this goal. The task is not a simple one.

Becker (1963:163–76) has discussed the problems encountered in studying deviants of various kinds. His observations are particularly applicable to crime. Becker suggests, for instance, that there are not enough studies of criminal behavior or of various kinds of criminal activity. Nor are the studies at present available adequate to the task of sociological theorizing, since they are superficial and hampered by sampling limitations and the like. Whether or not this has led to biased theories (i.e., inaccurate descriptions of the world) or has merely been instrumental in limiting criminology's conceptions of possible worlds is a debatable point the solution of which rests with philosophical as opposed to empirical inquiry. The reasons criminology has produced so few studies in this realm are not, however, to be disputed.

Since, as Becker suggests, criminal activity tends to be kept hidden by one means or another, students interested in doing research on burglars, for example, face considerable difficulty. First, they confront the problem of finding some criminals (burglars) to study. How can one locate a sufficient number of burglars for adequate research? If one relies on incarcerated or convicted individuals, the conclusions that can be drawn about them are limited to this category, for one can never be sure that people engaged in similar activity but who are not officially identified are like those interviewed in a penal setting (cf. Polsky, 1969:109–43).

Second, even if contact were to be made with individuals of this type, the researcher must still convince them that they pose no threat. As many a researcher has discovered, assurances of anonymity are rarely enough to convince even a willing subject to divulge all he knows.

Most of these problems are technical matters that can be overcome, although not without the expenditure of considerable effort. Yet even then the moral and ethical issues involved in studying criminals are still present to plague the sensitive scholar. Research considerations of this variety cannot, however, be ironed out simply by improving methodological techniques.

The problems encountered in investigating the agents of the state and others engaged in criminal labeling are not altogether different or less difficult than those faced when studying criminal types of persons. If criminologists are to broaden their experienced realities, if they are to expand the dimensions of their world, increased efforts along these lines will have to be made.

A principle of trial lawyers is to use the best evidence available. For criminologists, gaining the best available data is sometimes a more trying undertaking. Law-enforcement agencies, for example, are particularly reluctant to allow professional types to investigate their activities. In fact, this is why so few studies of the police can be found in the literature of criminology. If, for instance, one wishes to decipher how police officers make arrest decisions, it would be desirable to accompany them and observe them while engaged in this activity. It would be even better to experience directly what the police face by participating in the activity. Not only is it difficult to gain this kind of access, but even if one receives official sanction there is still no guarantee that one's subjects will speak and behave openly and freely in the presence of the researcher.

In other areas, different obstacles are encountered by the student who desires to reach the inner workings of judicial institutions. Jury behavior remains a dark area because juries have been protected from outside investigation by law. Judges, prosecutors, and defense attorneys shy away from letting some "radical" criminologist listen in on the backroom horsetrading that goes on in settling criminal cases. Also, tracing the legislative process can often be a tedious and futile experience, especially when legislators, lobbyists, and others are involved in a politically sensitive matter. In short, judicial authorities and political personages tend to be more inaccessible to research than are other bureaucratic or occupational groups. In many cases it is probably easier to research a group of practicing thieves than it is systematically to investigate the servants of law and political officers. The limited studies in this area are both testimony to scholarly dedication and examples of the closed-door nature of a significant arena for criminologic experience. What is amazing is not that there are so few studies but that there are any at all.

Again, most of the issues discussed here are technical in nature and are solvable. Given creativity, adequate academic preparation, and dedication, much can be discovered about the workings of judicial institutions. A number of criminologists are already working in this area, and several inroads have been made. But being able to observe and lacking the conceptual tools to comprehend what is observed make for a kind of intellectual blindness that plagues many an observer. Theoretic understanding and, hence, the world-as-known present infinite possibilities, limited only by one's vision and desire to look.

CONCLUSION

Sociology and its subfields, such as criminology, have constantly encountered the problem of justifying its existence. In part as a response to those who would discredit the sociological enterprise as useless, sociologists have devoted a good deal of effort to studying a proliferation of serious social issues in addition to seeking (without much success) to show sociology's usefulness by suggesting ways in which these problems can be remedied. Campus unrest, the ravages of poverty, unemployment, marital discord, drug addiction, and crime are but a few of the problems addressed by sociologists. Given that little has been done to ameliorate these situations, it is apparent that sociology has a long way to go before it can seriously proclaim its pragmatic value.

For those who care to listen, however, sociology does have something of great, if less tangible, value to offer. It can alert the student to alternative images of the world and alternative ways of looking at it. In this way sociology can act as a liberating science, freeing students from the bondage of their own conceptual limitations by awakening them to other possibilities. This is probably the major contribution sociologists, as sociologists, can hope to make. It is time that criminology shared more fully in this adventure.

References

ABRAHAMSEN, DAVID
  1945 *Crime and the Human Mind*, New York: Columbia University Press.
ADAMS, STUART
  1962 "The PICO Project," in Norman Johnson *et al.* (eds.), *The Sociology of Punishment and Corrections*, New York: John Wiley & Sons, pp. 213–24.
AKERS, RONALD L.
  1964 "Socio-Economic Status and Delinquent Behavior: A Retest," *Journal of Research in Crime and Delinquency, 1* (January): 38–46.
AMERICAN CORRECTIONAL ASSOCIATION
  1972 "The Development of Modern Correctional Concepts and Standards," in Robert M. Carter *et al., Correctional Institutions*, Philadelphia: Lippincott, pp. 17–34.
AUBERT, VILHELM, and SHELDON L. MESSINGER
  1958 "The Criminal and the Sick," *Inquiry, 1:* 137–60.
BARNES, HARRY E., and NEGLEY K. TEETERS
  1959 *New Horizons in Criminology*, 3rd ed., Englewood Cliffs, N. J.: Prentice-Hall.
BECKER, HOWARD S.
  1963 *Outsiders: Studies in the Sociology of Deviance*, New York: The Free Press of Glencoe.

1967   "Whose Side Are We On?" *Social Problems, 14* (Winter): 239–47.

BENJAMIN, ROGER W., and THEODORE B. PEDELISKI
1969   "The Minnesota Public Defender System and the Criminal Law Process," *Law and Society Review, 4* (November): 279–320.

BITTNER, EGON
1967   "The Police on Skid Row: A Study of Peace Keeping," *American Sociological Review, 32* (October): 699–715.

BLACK, DONALD J., and ALBERT J. REISS, JR.
1970   "Police Control of Juveniles," *American Sociological Review, 35* (February): 63–77.

BLOCH, HERBERT A., and GILBERT GEIS
1962   *Man, Crime, and Society,* New York: Random House.

BLUMBERG, ABRAHAM S.
1967   "The Practice of Law as Confidence Game: Organizational Coöptation of a Profession," *Law and Society Review, 1* (June): 15–39.

BORDUA, DAVID J., and ALBERT J. REISS, JR.
1966   "Command, Control, and Charisma: Reflections on Police Bureaucracy," *American Journal of Sociology, 72* (July): 68–76.

CALDWELL, ROBERT G.
1961   "The Juvenile Court: Its Development and Some Major Problems," *Journal of Criminal Law, Criminology, and Police Science, 51* (January–February): 493–511.

CARLIN, JEROME E.
1962   *Lawyers on Their Own: A Study of Individual Practitioners in Chicago,* New Brunswick, N. J.: Rutgers University Press.

CASPER, JONATHAN D.
1972   *American Criminal Justice: The Defendant's Perspective,* Englewood Cliffs, N. J.: Prentice-Hall.

CAVAN, RUTH SHONLE
1955   *Criminology,* 2nd. ed., New York: Thomas Y. Crowell.

CHAMBLISS, WILLIAM J.
1964   "A Sociological Analysis of the Law of Vagrancy," *Social Problems, 12* (Summer): 67–77.
1969   *Crime and the Legal Process,* New York: McGraw-Hill.

CLINARD, MARSHALL B. (ed.)
1964   *Anomie and Deviant Behavior,* New York: The Free Press of Glencoe.

CLINARD, MARSHALL B., and RICHARD QUINNEY
1967   *Criminal Behavior Systems: A Typology,* New York: Holt, Rinehart and Winston.

CLOWARD, RICHARD A.
1959   "Illegitimate Means, Anomie and Deviant Behavior," *American Sociological Review, 24* (April): 164–76.

CLOWARD, RICHARD A., and LLOYD OHLIN
1960 *Delinquency and Opportunity,* New York: The Free Press of Glencoe.

COHEN, ALBERT K.
1955 *Delinquent Boys,* New York: The Free Press of Glencoe.

COLE, GEORGE F.
1970 "The Decision to Prosecute," *Law and Society Review, 4* (February): 331–43.

COOLEY, CHARLES H.
1956 *Human Nature and the Social Order,* New York: The Free Press of Glencoe.

CRESSEY, DONALD
1953 *Other People's Money,* New York: The Free Press of Glencoe.
1960 "Epidemiology and Individual Conduct: A Case from Criminology," *Pacific Sociological Review, 3* (Fall): 47–58.

DAVIS, F. JAMES
1962 "Law as a Type of Social Control," in F. James Davis *et al.* (eds.), *Society and the Law: New Meanings for an Old Profession,* New York: The Free Press of Glencoe, pp. 39–63.

DeFLEUR, MELVIN, and RICHARD QUINNEY
1966 "A Reformulation of Sutherland's Differential Association Theory and a Strategy for Empirical Verification," *Journal of Research in Crime and Delinquency, 3* (January): 1–22.

DICKSON, DONALD T.
1968 "Bureaucracy and Morality: An Organizational Perspective on a Moral Crusade," *Social Problems, 16* (Fall): 143–56.

DOUGLAS, JACK D.
1967 *The Social Meanings of Suicide,* Princeton, N. J.: Princeton University Press.
1970 "Deviance and Respectability," in Jack D. Douglas (ed.), *Deviance and Respectability: The Social Construction of Moral Meanings,* New York: Basic Books, pp. 3–30.

DURKHEIM, EMILE
1947 *The Division of Labor in Society,* trans. by George Simpson, New York: The Free Press of Glencoe.
1951 *Suicide,* trans. by John A. Spaulding and George Simpson, New York: The Free Press of Glencoe.
1964 *The Rules of Sociological Method,* trans. by Sarah A. Solovay and John H. Mueller and ed. by George E. G. Catlin, New York: The Free Press.

ENGLAND, RALPH W.
1955 "A Study of Post-probation Recidivism Among Five Hundred Federal Offenders," *Federal Probation, 19* (September): 10–16.

ERIKSON, KAI T.
1964 "Notes on the Sociology of Deviance," in Howard S. Becker (ed.), *The Other Side,* New York: The Free Press, pp. 9–21.
1966 *Wayward Puritans,* New York: John Wiley and Sons.

ERIKSON, MAYNARD L., and LAMAR T. EMPEY
  1963   "Court Records, Undetected Delinquency, and Decision Making," *Journal of Criminal Law, Criminology, and Police Science, 54* (December): 456–69.

FEDERAL BUREAU OF INVESTIGATION
  1971   *Uniform Crime Reports, Crime in the United States,* Washington, D. C.: U. S. Government Printing Office.

FERDINARD, THEODORE N., and ELMER G. LUCHTERHAND
  1970   "Inner-City Youths, the Police, the Juvenile Court, and Justice," *Social Problems, 17* (Spring): 510–27.

FOX, RICHARD
  1971   "The XYY Offender: A modern Myth?" *Journal of Criminal Law, Criminology, and Police Science, 62* (March–April): 59–73.

GARFINKEL, HAROLD
  1956   "Conditions of Successful Degradation Ceremonies," *American Journal of Sociology, 61* (March): 420–24.

GAUDET, FREDERICK J.
  1933   "Individual Differences in the Sentencing Tendencies of Judges," *Journal of Criminal Law, Criminology, and Police Science, 23* (January): 811–18.

GIBBONS, DON C.
  1965   *Changing the Lawbreaker: The Treatment of Delinquents and Criminals,* Englewood Cliffs, N. J.: Prentice-Hall.
  1968   *Society, Crime, and Criminal Careers,* Englewood Cliffs, N. J.: Prentice-Hall.
  1969   "Crime and Punishment: A Study in Social Attitudes," *Social Forces, 47* (June): 391–97.
  1970   *Delinquent Behavior,* Englewood Cliffs, N. J.: Prentice-Hall.
  1971   "Observations on the Study of Crime Causation," *American Journal of Sociology, 77* (September): 262–78.
  n.d.   "Treatment Modalities, Corrections, and Rehabilitation," unpublished.

GIBBONS, DON C., and DONALD L. GARRITY
  1959   "Some Suggestions for the Development of Etiological and Treatment Theory in Criminology," *Social Forces, 38* (October): 51–58.

GIBBONS, DON C., and JOSEPH F. JONES
  1971   "Some Critical Notes on Current Definitions of Deviance," *Pacific Sociological Review, 14* (January): 20–37.

GIBBS, JACK P.
  1962   "Rates of Mental Hospitalization," *American Sociological Review, 27* (December): 782-92.

GLASER, DANIEL
  1964   *The Effectiveness of a Prison and Parole System,* Indianapolis, Ind.: Bobbs-Merrill.

1972   *Adult Crime and Social Policy,* Englewood Cliffs, N. J.: Prentice-Hall.

GLUECK, SHELDON, and ELEANOR GLUECK
1951   *Unraveling Juvenile Delinquency,* Cambridge, Mass.: Harvard University Press.

GOFFMAN, ERVING
1959   "The Moral Career of the Mental Patient," *Psychiatry, 23* (May): 123–31.
1963   *Stigma,* Englewood Cliffs, N. J.: Prentice-Hall.

GOLDMAN, NATHAN
1963   *The Differential Selection of Juvenile Offenders for Court Appearance,* New York: National Council on Crime and Delinquency.

GORING, CHARLES
1913   *The English Convict: A Statistical Study,* London: His Majesty's Stationery Office.

GREEN, EDWARD
1961   *Judicial Attitudes in Sentencing,* London: Macmillan.
1970   "Race, Social Status, and Criminal Arrest," *American Sociological Review, 35* (June): 476–90.

GUSFIELD, JOSEPH R.
1967   "Moral Passage: The Symbolic Process in Public Designations of Deviance," *Social Problems, 45* (Fall): 175–88.

HAKEEM, MICHAEL
1958   "A Critique of the Psychiatric Approach to Crime and Corrections," *Law and Contemporary Problems, 23* (Autumn): 650–82.

HALL, JEROME
1952   *Theft, Law, and Society,* 2nd ed., Indianapolis, Ind.: Bobbs-Merrill.

HANDERICH, TED
1971   *Punishment: The Supposed Justifications,* Baltimore, Md.: Penguin.

HARRIS, RICHARD
1969   *The Fear of Crime,* New York: Praeger.

HART, HENRY M., JR.
1958   "The Aims of the Criminal Law," *Law and Contemporary Problems, 23* (Summer): 401–41.

HARTJEN, CLAYTON A.
1972   "The Possibility of Crime: A Sociological Investigation of Cultural Grammar," Unpublished Ph.D. Dissertation, New York: New York University.
1972a "Police-Citizen Encounters: Social Order in Interpersonal Interaction," *Criminology, 10* (May): 61–84.
1972b "Legalism and Humanism: A Reply to the Schwendingers," *Issues in Criminology, 7* (Winter): 59–69.

HARTJEN, CLAYTON A., and DON C. GIBBONS
1969 "An Empirical Investigation of a Criminal Typology," *Sociology and Social Research, 54* (October): 56–62.

HINDELANG, MICHAEL J.
1970 "The Commitment of Delinquents to Their Misdeeds: Do Delinquents Drift?" *Social Problems, 17* (Spring): 502–9.

HOEBEL, E. ADAMSON
1954 *The Law of Primitive Man,* Cambridge, Mass.: Harvard University Press.

HOLZNER, BURKART
1968 *Reality Construction in Society,* Cambridge, Mass.: Schenkman.

HOOD, ROGER, and RICHARD SPARKS
1970 *Key Issues in Criminology,* New York: McGraw-Hill.

HOOTEN, EARNEST A.
1939 *Crime and the Man,* Cambridge, Mass.: Harvard University Press.

IRWIN, JOHN, and DONALD R. CRESSEY
1964 "Thieves, Convicts, and the Inmate Culture," in Howard S. Becker (ed.), *The Other Side,* New York: The Free Press, pp. 225–45.

JACKSON, BRUCE
1972 *Outside the Law: A Thief's Primer,* New Brunswick, N. J.: Transaction Books.

JEFFERY, C. RAY
1956 "The Structure of American Criminological Thinking," *Journal of Criminal Law, Criminology, and Police Science, 46* (January–February): 658–72.
1957 "The Development of Crime in Early English Society," *Journal of Criminal Law, Criminology, and Police Science, 47* (March–April): 647–66.

JENKINS, RICHARD L., and LESTER E. HEWITT
1944 "Types of Personality Structure Encountered in Child Guidance Clinics," *American Journal of Orthopsychiatry, 14* (January): 84–94.

JESNESS, CARL F.
1965 *The Fricot Ranch Study.* Sacramento: State of California, Department of the Youth Authority.

KALVEN, HARRY, JR., and HANS ZEISEL
1966 *The American Jury,* Boston: Little, Brown.

KAPLAN, JOHN
1973 *Criminal Justice: Introductory Cases and Materials,* Nincola, N. J.: Foundation Press.

KARLEN, DELMAR
1964 *The Citizen in Court,* New York: Holt, Rinehart, and Winston.

KINCH, JOHN W.
1962 "Continuities in the Study of Delinquent Types," *Journal of*

Criminal Law, Criminology, and Police Science, 53 (September–October): 323–28.

1962a "Self-Concepts of Types of Delinquents," *Sociological Inquiry, 32* (Spring): 228–34.

KITSUSE, I., and AARON CICOUREL

1963 "A Note on the Use of Official Statistics," *Social Problems, 11* (Fall): 131–39.

KITTRIE, NICHOLAS N.

1973 *The Right to Be Different: Deviance and Enforced Therapy,* Baltimore, Md.: Penguin.

KORN, RICHARD R., and LLOYD W. McCORKLE

1959 *Criminology and Penology,* New York: Holt, Rinehart, and Winston.

KOVAL, MARY

1971 "Differential Estimates of Narcotics Use in New York City," Unpublished, New York: State Narcotic Addiction Control Commission.

LaFAVE, WAYNE R.

1965 *Arrest: The Decision to Take a Suspect into Custody,* Boston: Little, Brown.

LANDER, BERNARD

1954 *Toward an Understanding of Juvenile Delinquency,* New York: Columbia University Press.

LEMERT, EDWIN M.

1951 *Social Pathology,* New York: McGraw-Hill.

1953 "An Isolation and Closure Theory of Naive Check Forgery," *Journal of Criminal Law, Criminology, and Police Science, 44* (September–October): 286–307.

LERMAN, PAUL

1968 "Evaluative Studies of Institutions for Delinquents: Implications for Research and Social Policy," *Social Work, 13* (July): 55–64.

LOFLAND, JOHN

1969 *Deviance and Identity,* Englewood Cliffs, N. J.: Prentice-Hall.

MALINOWSKI, BRONISLOW

1926 *Crime and Custom in Savage Society,* London: Routledge and Kegan Paul.

MATZA, DAVID

1964 *Delinquency and Drift,* New York: John Wiley and Sons.

1969 *Becoming Deviant,* Englewood Cliffs, N. J.: Prentice-Hall.

McCORKLE, LLOYD W., ALBERT ELLIS, and F. LOVELL BIXBY

1958 *The Highfields Story,* New York: Holt.

McCUNE, SHIRLEY D., and DANIEL L. SKOLER

1965 "Juvenile Court Judges in the United States," Part I: "A National Profile," *Crime and Delinquency, 11* (April): 121–31.

McHUGH, PETER

1970 "A Common-Sense Conception of Deviance," in Jack D. Douglas (ed.), *Deviance and Respectability: The Social Construction of Moral Meanings,* New York: Basic Books, pp. 61–88.

MEAD, GEORGE HERBERT
1934   *Mind, Self and Society,* Chicago: University of Chicago Press.

MERTON, ROBERT K.
1956   *Social Theory and Social Structure,* New York: Free Press.

MILLER, LOREN
1966   "Race, Poverty, and the Law," *California Law Review, 54* (May): 386–406.

MILLER, WALTER
1958   "Lower-Class Culture as a Generating Milieu of Gang Delinquency," *Journal of Social Issues, 14:* 5–19.

MORRIS, NORVAL
1966   "Impediments to Penal Reform," *University of Chicago Law Review, 33* (Summer): 627–56.

MUELLER, GERHARD O. W.
1955   "Tort, Crime and the Primitive," *Journal of Criminal Law, Criminology, and Police Science, 46* (September–October): 303–32.

NEWMAN, DONALD J.
1956   "Pleading Guilty for Consideration: A Study of Bargain Justice," *Journal of Criminal Law, Criminology, and Police Science, 46* (March–April): 780–90.
1957   "Public Attitudes Toward a Form of White-Collar Crime," *Social Problems, 4* (January): 228–32.

NIEDERHOFFER, ARTHUR
1969   *Behind the Shield,* Garden City, N. Y.: Doubleday.

PACKER, HERBERT L.
1968   *The Limits of the Criminal Sanction,* Stanford, Calif.: Stanford University Press.

PILIAVIN, IRVING, and SCOTT BRIAR
1964   "Police Encounters with Juveniles," *American Journal of Sociology, 70* (September): 206–14.

POLK, KENNETH
1957   "Juvenile Delinquency and Social Areas," *Social Problems, 5* (Winter): 214–17.

POLSKY, NED
1969   *Hustlers, Beats, and Others.* Garden City, N. Y.: Doubleday Anchor.

POUND, ROSCOE
1942   *Social Control Through Law,* New Haven, Conn.: Yale University Press.
1943   "A Survey of Social Interests," *Harvard Law Review, 57* (October): 1–39.

1959 *An Introduction to the Philosophy of Law*, New Haven, Conn.: Yale University Press.

PRESIDENT'S COMMISSION ON LAW ENFORCEMENT AND ADMINISTRATION OF JUSTICE
1967 *The Challenge of Crime in a Free Society*, Washington, D. C.: U. S. Government Printing Office.
1967a *Task Force Report: The Courts*, Washington, D. C.: U. S. Government Printing Office.

QUINNEY, RICHARD
1964 "Crime, Delinquency, and Social Areas," *Journal of Research in Crime and Delinquency, 1* (July): 149–54.
1970 *The Problem of Crime*, New York: Dodd, Mead.
1970a *The Social Reality of Crime*, Boston: Little, Brown.
1971 "Introduction," in Nicholas M. Regush, *The Drug Addiction Business*, New York: Dial, pp. ix–xiii.
1972 "The Ideology of Law: Notes for a Radical Alternative to Legal Oppression," *Issues in Criminology, 7* (Winter): 1–35.
1973 "Crime Control in Capitalist Society: A Critical Philosophy of Legal Order," *Issues in Criminology, 1* (Spring): 75–99.

REISS, ALBERT J., JR.,
1951 "Delinquency as the Failure of Personal and Social Control," *American Sociological Review, 16* (April): 196–208.

REISS, ALBERT J., JR., and ALBERT LEWIS RHODES
1961 "The Distribution of Delinquency in the Social Class Structure," *American Sociological Review, 26* (October): 720–32.

REIWALD, PAUL
1949 *Society and Its Criminals*, trans. and ed. by T. E. James, London: Heinemann.

ROBY, PAMELA A.
1969 "Politics and Criminal Law: Revision of the New York State Penal Law on Prostitution," *Social Problems, 17* (Summer): 83–109.

ROEBUCK, JULIAN B.
1966 *Criminal Typology*, New York: Thomas Y. Crowell.

ROONEY, ELIZABETH A., and DON C. GIBBONS
1966 "Social Reactions to Crimes Without Victims," *Social Problems, 13* (Spring): 400-10.

ROSE, ARNOLD M., and ARTHUR E. PRELL
1955 "Does the Punishment Fit the Crime? A Study in Social Valuation," *American Journal of Sociology, 61* (November): 247–59.

ROSEN, LAWRENCE, and STANLEY H. TURNER
1967 "An Evaluation of the Lander Approach to Ecology of Delinquency," *Social Problems, 15* (Fall): 189–200.

SAVITZ, LEONARD
1967 *Dilemmas in Criminology*, New York: McGraw-Hill.

SCHNUR, ALFRED C.
1958 "The New Penology, Fact or Fiction?" *Journal of Criminal Law, Criminology, and Police Science, 49* (November–December): 331–34.
1958a "Some Reflections on the Role of Correctional Research," *Law and Contemporary Problems, 23* (April): 722-873.

SCHUESSLER, KARL E.
1952 "The Deterrent Influence of the Death Penalty," *Annals, 284* (November): 54–63.

SCHUR, EDWIN M.
1968 *Law and Society: A Sociological View,* New York: Random House.
1969 *Our Criminal Society,* Englewood Cliffs, N. J.: Prentice-Hall.

SCHWARTZ, RICHARD D., and JEROME H. SKOLNICK
1964 "Two Studies of Legal Stigma," in Howard S. Becker (ed.), *The Other Side,* New York: The Free Press: pp. 103–17.

SCHWENDINGER, HERMAN, and JULIA SCHWENDINGER
1970 "Defenders of Order or Guardians of Human Rights?" *Issues in Criminology, 5* (Summer): 123–57.

SELLIN, THORSTEN
1938 *Culture Conflict and Crime,* New York: Social Science Research Council.
1958 "Corrections in Historical Perspective," *Law and Contemporary Problems, 23* (Autumn): 585–93.

SHAW, CLIFFORD R., and HENRY D. McKAY
1929 *Delinquent Areas,* Chicago: University of Chicago Press.
1942 *Juvenile Delinquency and Urban Areas,* Chicago: University of Chicago Press.

SHAW, CLIFFORD R., HENRY D. McKAY, and JAMES F. McDONALD
1938 *Brothers in Crime,* Chicago: University of Chicago Press.

SHELDON, WILLIAM H., S. S. STEVENS, and W. B. TUCKER
1949 *Varieties of Delinquent Youth,* New York: Harper and Row.

SHORT, JAMES F., JR., and F. IVAN NYE
1958 "Extent of Unrecorded Juvenile Delinquency: Tentative Conclusions," *Journal of Criminal Law, Criminology, and Police Science, 49* (November–December): 296-302.

SILVERSTEIN, LEE
1965 *Defense of the Poor in Criminal Cases,* Chicago: American Bar Foundation.

SKOLNICK, JEROME H.
1966 *Justice Without Trial,* New York: John Wiley and Sons.

SMIGEL, ERWIN O.
1953 "Public Attitudes Toward 'Chiseling' With Reference to Unemployment Compensation," *American Sociological Review, 18* (February): 59–67.
1956 "Public Attitudes Toward Stealing as Related to Size of Victim

Organization," *American Sociological Review, 21* (June): 320–27.

STRAUS, ROBERT
n.d. "Social Change and the Rehabilitation Concept," in Marvin B. Sussman (ed.), *Sociology and Rehabilitation*, a publication of the American Sociological Association, pp. 1–34.

STRODTBECK, FRED, and L. H. HOOK
1961 "The Social Dimensions of the Twelve-Man Jury Trial," *Sociometry, 24* (December): 397–415.

STRODTBECK, FRED, R. M. JAMES, and J. C. HAWKINS
1957 "Social Status and Jury Deliberations," *American Sociological Review, 22* (December): 713–19.

SUDNOW, DAVID
1965 "Normal Crimes: Sociological Features of the Penal Code in a Public Defender Office," *Social Problems, 12* (Winter): 255–76.

SULLIVAN, CLYDE E., MARGUERITE Q. GRANT, and DOUGLAS J. GRANT
1957 "The Development of Interpersonal Maturity: Applications to Delinquency," *Psychiatry, 20*: 373–85.

SUTHERLAND, EDWIN H.
1937 *The Professional Thief*, Chicago: University of Chicago Press.
1949 *White Collar Crime*, New York: Holt, Rinehart and Winston.
1950 "The Sexual Psychopath Laws," *Journal of Criminal Law, Criminology, and Police Science, 40* (January–February): 543–54.
1950a "The Diffusion of Sexual Psychopath Laws," *American Journal of Sociology, 56* (September): 142–48.

SUTHERLAND, EDWIN H., and DONALD R. CRESSEY
1966 *Principles of Criminology*, 7th. ed., Philadelphia: J. B. Lippincott.

SYKES, GRESHAM M.
1958 *The Society of Captives*, New York: Atheneum.

SYKES, GRESHAM M., and DAVID MATZA
1957 "Techniques of Neutralization: A Theory of Delinquency," *American Sociological Review, 22* (December): 664–70.

SZASZ, THOMAS S.
1970 "Involuntary Mental Hospitalization: A Crime Against Humanity," in Thomas S. Szasz (ed.), *Ideology and Insanity*, Garden City, N. Y.: Doubleday Anchor, pp. 113–39.

TANNENBAUM, FRANK
1938 *Crime and the Community*, Boston, Mass.: Ginn and Co.

TAPPAN, PAUL W.
1947 "Who Is the Criminal?" *American Sociological Review, 12* (February): 96–102.
1949 *Juvenile Delinquency*, New York: McGraw-Hill.
1960 *Crime, Justice and Correction*, New York: McGraw-Hill.

THORSELL, BERNARD A., and LLOYD W. KLEMKE
1972 "The Labeling Process: Reinforcement and Deterrent," *Law and Society Review, 6* (February): 393–403.

TITTLE, CHARLES R., and CHARLES H. LOGAN
1972 "Sanctions and Deviance: Evidence and Remaining Questions," *Law and Society Review, 7* (Spring): 371–93.

TURK, AUSTIN T.
1966 "Conflict and Criminality," *American Sociological Review, 31* (June): 338–52.
1969 *Criminology and Legal Order,* Chicago: Rand McNally.

VOLD, GEORGE B.
1958 *Theoretical Criminology,* New York: Oxford University Press.

WALD, PATRICIA
1967 "Poverty and Criminal Justice," in The President's Commission on Law Enforcement and Administration of Justice, *Task Force Report: The Courts,* Washington, D. C.: U. S. Government Printing Office, pp. 139–51.

WALLERSTEIN, JAMES S., and CLEMENT J. WYLE
1947 "Our Law-Abiding Law-Breakers," *Probation, 25* (April): 107–12.

WALTHER, REGIS H., and SHIRLEY D. McCUNE
1965 "Juvenile Court Judges in the United States," Part II: "Working Styles and Characteristics," *Crime and Delinquency, 11* (October): 384–93.

WHEELER, STANTON
1969 "Socialization in Correctional Institutions," in David A. Geslin (ed.), *Handbook of Socialization Theory and Research,* Chicago: Rand McNally, pp. 105–23.

WILSON, JAMES Q.
1968 *Varieties of Police Behavior,* Cambridge, Mass.: Harvard University Press.
1968a "The Police and the Delinquent in Two Cities," in Stanton Wheeler (ed.), *Controlling Delinquents,* New York: John Wiley and Sons, pp. 9–30.

WOLFGANG, MARVIN E.
1958 *Patterns of Criminal Homicide,* Philadelphia: University of Pennsylvania Press.

WOOD, ARTHUR L.
1967 *Criminal Lawyer,* New Haven, Conn.: College and University Press.

ZUCKERMANN, STANLEY B., ALFRED J. BARRON, and HORACE B. WHITTIER
1953 "A Follow-up Study of Minnesota State Reformatory Inmates," *Journal of Criminal Law, Criminology, and Police Science, 43* (January–February): 622–36.

Index